HURRY LESS WORRY LESS

HURRY LESS
WORRY LESS

10 Strategies for Living the Life You Long For

JUDY PACE CHRISTIE

DIMENSIONS
FOR LIVING
NASHVILLE

HURRY LESS, WORRY LESS
10 STRATEGIES FOR LIVING THE LIFE YOU LONG FOR

Copyright © 2005 by Judy Pace Christie

This book is printed on acid-free paper.

Library of Congress Cataloging-in-Publication Data

Christie, Judy Pace, 1956-
  Hurry less, worry less : 10 strategies for living the life you long for / Judy Pace Christie.
    p. cm.
  ISBN 0-687-06259-4 (pbk. : alk. paper)
  1. Time management—Religious aspects—Christianity. 2. Leisure—Religious aspects—Christianity. 3. Peace of mind—Religious aspects—Christianity. I. Title.
  BV4598.5.C47 2005
  248.4—dc22

2004029166

Scripture quotations, unless otherwise indicated, are taken from the HOLY BIBLE, NEW INTERNATIONAL VERSION®. NIV®. Copyright © 1973, 1978, 1984 by International Bible Society. Used by permission of Zondervan Publishing House. All rights reserved.

Scripture marked KJV is from the King James or Authorized Version of the Bible.

Quotation on page 51 is from MAKING ALL THINGS NEW: AN INVITATION TO THE SPIRITUAL LIFE by HENRI J.M. NOUWEN. Copyright © 1981 by Henri J.M. Nouwen. Reprinted by permission of HarperCollins Publishers Inc.

Quotation on page 61 is from Wendy Miller, *Invitation to a Presence: A Guide to Spiritual Disciplines* (Nashville: Upper Room Books, 1995).

Quotation on page 95 is from Ellen Gilchrist, *Falling Through Space* (1987). Used by permission.

Quotation on page 103 taken from *My Utmost for His Highest* by Oswald Chambers, copyright © 1935 by Dodd Mead & Co., renewed © 1963 by the Oswald Chambers Publications Assn. Ltd. Used by permission of Discovery House Publishers, Box 3566, Grand Rapids MI 49501. All rights reserved.

05 06 07 08 09 10 11 12 13 14—10 9 8 7 6 5 4 3 2 1

MANUFACTURED IN THE UNITED STATES OF AMERICA

In loving memory of my wonderful mother,

Betty Brosette Pace

CONTENTS

WITH GRATITUDE

*A*s I complete this book, it is a beautiful spring day outside and my heart is filled with thankfulness—to our loving God, who guides us to better places, and to the many people who helped me along the way. My cup runneth over!

Special thanks go to the many friends who have encouraged me through the years and who have prayed for me all along the way, not only during the writing of this book, but also during the entire journey—my tremendous Baylor FunFest friends who are such a part of me: Ginger Hamilton, Carol Lovelady and her husband, Sam, Gaye Slomka, Karen Enriquez, Peggy Camerino, Nancy Thompson, Laura Kimball, Laura Nolen, and Annette Boyd; my dear, loving friends, Kathie Rowell, Freda Jones, Rita Hummingbird, Sarah Plunkett, Marilyn Mitchell, Althea Goodwin, and Alisa Stingley, whose early editing and feedback made this book so much better; my spectacular SUMC Big Ham Small Group: Diane Dixon, Diane Byrum, Sami Bolger, Karen Fratterola, Linda Krager, and Sally Norman; and my *Times OC* pals who have been so incredibly supportive of my adventures: Cilla Trenado, Mary Hanisee, Sue Sirmons, Barb Deane, and Diana Barber.

Thanks, too, to Kathy "Birdie" Turner and Terri Hill, among the first to critique the idea for this book; Tammy

Warren, who offered great insight and coaching at a critical part of my journey; and Karen Shideler and Jim Wilson, office neighbors and friends who helped me stay focused on writing.

My life has been shaped in so many ways for decades by my wonderful church families at Parkview Baptist Church, Suntree United Methodist Church, and Grace Community Methodist Church. My love and heartfelt thanks go to all of you, with special thanks to Gary Spencer and Rob Weber, two terrific and wise pastors who continue to teach me so much and who are such wonderful leaders.

In every endeavor I've undertaken through the years, I have depended on the love and support of my family, the Pace boys, and their families. To Jack and Jane, Steve and Cid, David and Isabelle, and all their kids, I say a huge thanks with love. Then, along came the Christies, a wonderful new family I was blessed with in my midthirties, including Suzanne, Gracie, John, dear Jackie, Mary Frances, and my late mother-in-law, Eva Barnhill Christie.

And, finally, my never-ending love and thanks to my husband, Paul, who reminds me to "simplify, simplify" and who has been incredibly supportive as I have tried new things and learned to hurry less and worry less. I am so blessed to be married to you!

Introduction

Where Do You Start?

A few years ago I became desperate to regain control of my life. The decision came somewhere between running to the cleaners to pick up clothes on my way to the airport for a business trip, driving at 3 A.M. in a rental car to meet friends for what was supposed to be a restful weekend, and mailing yet another birthday gift late.

My life was so hectic, so rushed, so noisy that I did not know where to start. The demands of work and home and a million activities weighed on me. I was not sure it was possible to live at a slower pace. I certainly did not know many people who were doing so. Instead, I knew many people who, like me, were hungry to slow down their lives and enjoy life more. I could find few who had figured out how.

Perhaps you know the feeling: worn out, burned out, frazzled. Your personal cruise control seems always to be set on 80 or above. Everything is done in a hurry with a pretty good dose of worry to go along with it. You may very likely feel as though you do not have time to read this book, much less to learn how to hurry less. Slowing down seems impossible, short of running away from home.

When the desire to change hit me, I felt that I was in quicksand. I had a great job, wonderful friends, and a loving family, but, like a car that will not quite go into gear, something was out of sync. Part of me felt guilty for not being satisfied. Surely lots of people would be happy to have my life. I also felt vaguely uneasy about beginning to think about changing. What if I made the wrong decision or did something foolish?

The uneasiness and guilt and fear caused me to realize that hurry was only part of the problem with my life. It had a big evil twin called worry; they worked hand in hand and robbed me of daily pleasures. Too often I did not enjoy the blessings and good things in my life for anticipating problems or worrying about what I needed to do next.

Short of slamming on the brakes and refusing to get out of bed one day, I did not know where to start. That realization brought me to the best decision of all: I would start somewhere.

Maybe you feel the way I did—eager to make a change but unsure how to start. Take heart. You can make your life more closely resemble your hopes and dreams. Struggling along my journey, I collected and tried out hundreds of ideas that became tools for me. I offer them to you because I experienced how they can work. You will find that this is not merely about being more organized or managing time better. It is about transforming your life.

This book shares the path that I took and is written with the certainty that there is a better way to live, even in these hectic times—*especially* in these hectic times. My life is still exceedingly full, but it feels much better. I learned that it is possible to be dedicated and good at what I do and still live in a balanced way. This is not an either-or choice, but rather a blend. The strategies can be tackled in five- and ten-minute pieces as you have time.

An unexpected part of the journey was how God began to speak to me and help me grow, reminding me regularly that hurry and worry were not in the plans for me. God began to thaw parts of me I did not even realize were frozen. Even though I had been too busy to spend much time on spiritual matters, God was still there. I discovered that part of the yearning inside me was for this underdeveloped part of my life.

My hope is that my experiences will be helpful both for those who are active in their faith and feel a strong connection to God, and also for those of you who might not have given spiritual matters a second thought since second grade.

Once I decided I would try to change, almost miraculous things started to happen—and I believe that will be true for you, too. I was nearly relentless in my quest, finding it hard to approach tranquility in a tranquil way. The process sometimes felt as if I were taking three steps forward and two steps back—but, amazingly, I was still moving forward. God guided me in remarkable—and reassuring—ways. I had only to open the blinds a crack for light to shine in.

To all who need a nudge, I encourage you to consider the simplest of strategies: Decide you will give change a try. Take a look at the various chapters in this book and choose ideas that work for you. Adapt them. Create your own. You are the unique creation of a loving God who has wonderful plans for you—yes, even hurried, worried you.

You *can* live and work more meaningfully. Enjoy the journey!

Chapter One

What Do You Long For?

Encouraging Word: *You can slow down your life.*
Everyday Step: *Jot down a list of words you would like to describe your life.*

Hurry belongs to the evil one.—Ancient Arabian proverb

*M*any of us dash from one activity to another, worrying all the while about what else we should be doing. We need simple and practical ways to begin to change, ideas that work with our busy schedules. Despite many good things in our lives and various kinds of success, nothing seems quite right. We are stressed, tense, and fretful—about money, work, schedules, children, relationships, and the future. Daily we struggle, frantically trying to balance work and home.

When we pause for even a moment, we realize deep inside that this is not the way God intended for us to spend our precious days—nor the way we planned to live our lives.

Amazingly, here—in our craziest, busiest moments—is where we decide to live more fully. It starts with a tiny thought.

Now and then, we let ourselves wonder—sometimes for just a moment or two—if our lives could be different. Could we enjoy each day more? In our rush, we decide fairly quickly that we can't slow down. Other people might be able to change their lives, but not us. We are too busy to learn how to slow down, too worried to relax.

Be encouraged. You can change. Life can be more meaningful, less hurried and less worried, even for you. The most frenzied person can learn to slow down and find more peace and pleasure in life.

You can begin to change almost immediately—yes, even you, the person who feels like he or she does not have time to be reading this book. Quick and specific steps can help shape the life you are meant to live, not the one into which you have somehow slid.

These techniques can work in your busy, everyday world by taking one step at a time to a calmer and more enjoyable way of life. You do not have to hide under the bed or run away from home.

Using "Found Moments"

Slowing your life down can actually start on the run. It can be done by grabbing "found moments," a minute or two here and there. These can happen in the car, while you wait at the bank, in the fast-food drive-through, or on your way to work.

These found moments are not big blocks of time but are minutes you can grab to think and plan. They will become part of the road map for your journey toward an increased enjoyment of life. You will not change totally in one day—nor should you expect to. Such unrealistic expectations will only add more pressure and throw you off balance. This does not have to be yet another thing added to a to-do list. Instead, start with a few minutes where you envision the life you want.

Because you are so swamped most of the time, making

your life more enjoyable may seem to increase your stress at first. This feeling will fade as you choose specific strategies that work for you.

NEXT STEP: Develop a basic idea of what you want your life to look like.

Imagining your ideal life sometimes starts with knowing what you do *not* want your life to look like—knowing you are tired of being tired all the time or of rushing everywhere or feeling as if you never spend enough time with your family. That can lead to thinking about what you would like for your life to be like instead.

In my life, I found this to be a bit tougher than it sounds, for a couple of reasons. We get stuck living a certain way, and it is hard to step back. Taking a fresh look to see if we should change can seem overwhelming. Maybe you feel too busy and too tired to figure out why you are so busy and so tired. Even so, many of us have a pretty good idea about what we long for in our lives.

Your ideal life may be buried fairly deep under laundry, junk mail on the kitchen table, a stack of last week's newspapers, or a year's worth of unread magazines, or maybe even shoved down under a list of regrets. But many of us have "if only" lists that pop into our minds from time to time. We know that we would like to be calmer or have more fun or be joyful or have meaningful work.

Figuring out what I wanted my life to look like took me awhile. I read, studied, talked to friends and family, prayed, wondered—in between rushing about my daily life, working long hours, trying to be a good wife, mom, sister, aunt, friend, and on and on. What I eventually came up with certainly was not as complicated as brain surgery. I simply wanted less hurry and less worry in my life and more fun times spent with people I care about. And, I wanted to do work that has meaning. Those simple sentences are distilled from thousands of words and much reflection.

When I set out, I was rushing from one thing to another without truly enjoying any of it to the fullest. I yearned to change. I surprised myself when I sat down to write some goals. The words that came forth had a different tone than I expected: "More balance in all things. Slow down and enjoy life more by balancing work and play, togetherness and aloneness, planning and spontaneity, spending and saving, fitness of body and soul." At first my thoughts came together on the run. They eventually helped me slow down to give them more attention and do some fine-tuning.

The easiest way to get started is to jot down a list of words to describe your ideal life. You might write something such as, "I want these words to describe my life . . ." and list the words. This simple exercise, which takes only a few minutes, begins to help you form one-word goals that can move you along, even on the busiest days.

During this process, you are already changing. You are finding moments in your busy schedule to think differently and beginning to acknowledge that you might be able to live differently.

Perhaps you would like to be more serene, loving, spiritual, or organized. Maybe you want your life to be more purposeful. Maybe you want to move slower each day or quit waking up worried in the night. The words you choose are not magic, but they help you start moving toward enjoying life more. The very act of writing these words down helps you make conscious, positive steps in the right direction. They can be nouns or adjectives, phrases or sentences. Do not get hung up on the form. This is your life, and this is your list.

As I started to list such words, I was surprised when the word *tranquil* popped into my mind. It was not a word I had thought about before, and it was the opposite of the noisy, frenzied life I tended to live. It became sort of a touchstone for me, reminding me of the quieter, more fulfilling life I craved. Other words that appealed to me included *integrity, generosity,* and *usefulness.* I offer this list to help you get started, but choose words that fit you and your dreams.

Remember, these are not words that describe your life now, but words that describe the way you would like for your life to be.

A church group I worked with in Florida listed *joyful, serene, reflective, patient, fulfilling, loving, productive, spiritual, organized,* and *peaceful.* These were words they wanted to build their lives around. A group of journalism executives gave nearly the same list, adding *meaningful* and *fun.* A small group of working women in Louisiana again chose very similar words. Most groups want these words to replace words such as *anxious, tired, hurried, harried, rushed, frenzied, busy*—the words they think their children, spouses, or friends would too often use to describe them.

The similarities in lists from different groups remind me that most of those I bump into day in and day out want the same things I want. At first, I found this to be sobering. How, how, how had we let our lives get so out of control? Later, I found this to be encouraging. As we try to retool our daily routines, we have comrades in our war—and oftentimes an angel or two.

Possibility Words

As you begin, do not make a list that reflects a lot of "shoulds" for your life, words that may reflect what other people want you to do. Make a list that comes from within you—possibility words that express your thoughts and dreams. Begin to think about these words while you are driving or sitting in traffic or waiting for the carpool kids to hop into your minivan.

Consider buying a notebook or journal and using it to capture your thoughts in one place as you take steps toward achieving less hurry and worry. This notebook can become an inspiration for you as you move forward. Having a separate notebook where I jotted thoughts kept me reminded of my journey and on down the road showed me how far I had come. However, do not fret about where you write it—a tablet, napkin, scrap of paper, or the margin of this book can work, too.

Your life is fluid, and your list probably will not be static—especially at first. This process is not like filling out a tax form or a sweepstakes entry blank. Instead, it offers you plenty of freedom to quit thinking about "ought tos" and begin to think about "want tos." Some people might have a dozen words that pop into mind. They will quickly focus on these. Others might have one or two that will help shape their lives.

Some folks do well when they take out a piece of paper and begin to download their brains, jotting every word that pops up. The list can be edited later and take its life-changing shape. You might want to ask a good friend for feedback on your list. Does he or she notice something missing that you have mentioned before? This discussion with a friend or family member does not need a formal retreat setting. You can do it over lunch or while watching a children's soccer game or by e-mail. And, maybe your friend will want to make a list of his or her own and swap ideas.

Matching Your Life to Your Words

You have taken the first step to enjoying each day to the fullest by beginning to consider what you want your life to look like. Now, you can begin to consider what you might do to help your life match those words. As you go about your daily life, remember that list of words.

TRY THIS: Focus on one word each day.

Tape your list of words on your bathroom mirror or put it on your desk at work. Choose words from your list for passwords for your computer. Pray about or meditate on the words. When you consider these words, you are really considering how to transform your life.

Begin to recall those words as you make decisions in your daily life—even small decisions. Does the decision help your life look the way you want it to or does it take you down a road you would rather not travel?

Taking Baby Steps Toward Slowing Down

Begin to be aware that you can stop rushing so much and each day take baby steps toward slowing down. If you want to have more time with your family in the evenings, for example, you probably don't want to sign up for that night class right now or volunteer for a committee that has regular night meetings. If you are tired of rushing, you may want to leave home a little earlier each morning, instead of throwing that load of laundry in at the last minute or straightening all the rugs before you walk out the door. You may choose to read a book rather than watch a noisy TV show, or you may decide to walk around the block with your spouse after supper rather than spend an hour on the computer.

Diverting Negative Thoughts

These small steps help you gain momentum and slowly begin to make bigger decisions about living the way you want to each day. You may find that you turn down a new job that would require extra hours or that you set aside time to get your master's degree so you can start your own business.

As you begin to consider retooling your life—even with one small thought or a simple list of words—it may seem like an entire ugly family has moved into your brain, each with little voices trying to pull you offtrack. One voice wants you to believe you are failing because you can't do everything. Or maybe you hear a voice telling you that you must hurry all the time; that is just the way life is. Or, a voice tells you to buckle down, work harder, never exercise, eat lots of junk food, and drink too much coffee. The worst voice that many clients have mentioned to me is that middle-of-the-night voice that finds you lying awake worrying about all manner of things.

Try not to pay attention to these negative thoughts. You are creating a new way of living. Learning to relax and quiet these voices is part of moving forward. When you find yourself fretting over something you think you should have done or worrying about what is going to happen next month, divert the thoughts. Consider instead ways you might enjoy life more.

From the small seeds you have planted with these words, new ideas will begin to sprout and some amazing things may blossom. Slowly, the words begin to help you connect the dots and give you a glimpse of the Big Picture of what you want your life to look like—an inspiring, more exciting look at your life. Using the Big Picture as a foundation, you can begin to focus on your priorities.

Slowly, you will find that you have more time to spend on making fundamental changes in your perspective and actions. This process is somewhat like keeping the checkbook balanced or staying in shape. It will take attention, but it will work. You will begin to sense ways to slow down and be more effective in your work and at home.

Not a One-size-fits-all Fix

Choosing strategies to live more meaningfully is not a one-size-fits-all proposition. You will custom design strategies to fit your life and your hopes for the future. The demands on us, while similar, are also oddly individual. We are all called to live our unique lives to the fullest.

After you capture words for your life on paper, you might begin to write about those words to see what bubbles to the top. Again, you do not have to have hours to do this. Simply take your paper out while you are waiting somewhere and let your thoughts flow. Most of us do not want to give up sleep for anything, but you might consider getting up 15 to 30 minutes earlier or staying up later as this process unfolds—making a short-term sacrifice for long-term change.

The important part of moving toward change is not how much time you put into it, but that you begin to move forward—one small step at a time.

A TIP: This is a good time to think about people you know or have known who have lived their lives in ways you admire.

What did they do that you would like to emulate? How did they make it work? My Aunt Jean had a strong sense of family and home, was kind and funny, loved to go and do, but also had a serenity about her. The sewing-and-cooking wife of a soybean farmer, she married as a teenager and raised her family in the Mississippi Delta. In thinking about her, I realized it was not her day-to-day life that I wanted to copy—it was her spirit, her manner. She possessed qualities that I wanted to permeate my personal life and my work. As I became aware of those, I found myself trying to exhibit more of them.

ANOTHER STRATEGY: Write down your ideal work week. Since most of us work outside the home these days, we *must* learn how to blend our home and work lives.

In my own life and in working with hundreds of people, I have found that being able to balance work and home does not happen without awareness. Most people I talk to work *hard* each day. Some days it feels as though someone has walked on our brains with cleats by the time we head home. Too often we are left without much energy or enthusiasm for the family and the evening ahead.

My ideal work week includes planning to prevent rushing, allowing time to get where I'm going without my heart rate and my speedometer going too high. It includes setting time for projects that need to be done, so they don't wind up attacking me at week's end. It means staying a step ahead, instead of procrastinating and falling a step behind.

No matter what kind of work you do—management, clerical, medical, the endless list of possibilities—consider some specifics of an ideal week and begin to use them as the scaffolding for building a life you enjoy more each day. I have led many businesspeople through this exercise, watching them realize ways they can do their jobs better, get home earlier, and take the strain out of mundane chores.

Many of us enjoyed our work until we got so busy. This step helps rekindle some of that pleasure from work.

What Do You Long For?

We are impatient. We are used to drive-through food, drive-through banks, drive-through pharmacies. We honk when the car in front of us does not make a jackrabbit start the instant the light changes. We try to tell our spouse the quicker route to wherever we happen to be going. Students in classes I have taught on this topic admit to an addiction to hurry—even when they might not have to hurry. This addiction does not have to be permanent. We can learn to schedule fewer things, plan fewer activities, do more of the "coulds" and fewer of the "shoulds."

At Christmastime, a gardener friend was raving about her beautiful blooming amaryllis plant, so my husband and I bought what seemed like a rather expensive bulb and planted it, expecting the huge red blossom to pop out right in time for the family Christmas gathering. Christmas came and went; New Year's Day came and went; Valentine's Day got closer, but still no bloom. That plant was moving along at its own pace. After what seemed like weeks in the dirt, the tiniest of leaves inched out, slowly shooting higher and higher. Then came buds, which stayed tightly shut for days longer. Finally, the bloom burst forth—beautiful, extravagant, downright exciting. It had gone through each of the necessary steps. So it is in our own lives. We have gotten so busy that we want to see the bloom today.

Do not give up when your life does not immediately become what you hope for. Keep at this steady process. The journey has begun, and from that beginning will certainly come the changes you seek. Expect good things. Be an optimist. Open your heart and soul to this process.

Chapter Two

CREATE A NEW ROAD MAP FOR YOUR LIFE

Encouraging Word: *God is most willing to help us get started on this journey—even if we've been too busy for spiritual matters for quite some time.*
Everyday Step: *Stop, if only briefly, to get your bearings and catch your breath.*

First say to yourself what you would be, and then do what you have to do.—Epictetus

*S*ome years back, a girlfriend and I decided to drive to San Diego to visit another friend. We made the long journey, halfway across the country, with little trouble—until we took a wrong exit on the interstate within miles of our destination. We got so turned around within minutes that we could not even figure out how to get back to the highway. The harder we tried, the more confused we became. That is the way a frenzied life can begin to feel—as though we have traveled a long way only to be hopelessly lost. We are tired and irritable and want to be somewhere else.

Not knowing where we are is a frustrating, aggravating, and sometimes even scary experience. When we find ourselves in a place we do not want to be, we can use the same thing we do when we lose our way on a trip: We ask for directions and pull out a road map to show us the way. We think about where we made a wrong turn and how to get back on the road we want to be on.

One way or the other, we must stop and get our bearings. This is how we plan our journey to a renewed and refreshed life.

Two of my favorite computer tools are online maps and directions. Type in where you are and where you want to wind up, and it will plot it out for you instantly—including the estimated time to get there and the twists and turns along the way. This journey that you are embarking on is somewhat like that—except you get to create your own map to help you find where you want to be. This is where you move a bit further down the road on the path that best suits you—determined to see new things, perhaps visit old favorite spots, break away for adventure, or savor long-forgotten pleasures.

Attack of the "Second-thoughts Syndrome"

Reconsidering Taking the Trip

By now, you may be reconsidering taking the trip at all. Maybe you realize you have been headed down the wrong road but just do not have the energy to change directions. Maybe, you think, it would be better to backtrack later than try to change directions now. The Second-thoughts Syndrome has jumped on you with full force. You decide that change is not possible in your chaotic world, that you are not an introspective or spiritual person, that you have bills to pay and children to chauffeur and projects to do at work and on and on. You get tired just thinking about it. Sometimes we wake up feeling like the tide of life has swept us so far away from where we want to be, and we do not have the stamina to go against that tide. Take heart. This process is a journey. It includes preparation, planning, and probably the occasional U-turn, but it does not have to be complicated. Interesting thoughts will pop up as you go, and experiences will give you energy. The scenery will become increasingly captivating.

AT THIS STAGE: Do not forget to pray for traveling mercies.

To get from where you are in your daily life to the point where you are meant to be requires prayer. "Uh-oh," you say. "I don't really know how to pray," or "I haven't prayed in years" or "I would not know where to start." Put your foot on the brake and stop obsessing about all those concerns. You can learn to ask for God's guidance in your daily life. As I started down this path, not knowing if I could really hurry less, I slowly began to get a new sense of God's presence in my life. I learned new ways to pray—despite my crazy schedule and noisy life. From that came a renewed sense of how wonderful God wants my life to be. This certainly did not start as a spiritual journey. I lumped it originally into a more generic "lifestyle" category. But I was surprised at how willing God was to help me get started changing my life. I realized that God would walk with me every step of the way, even if I had been so busy that I had given too little thought to God for quite some time.

Asking for Help

Asking God to show you the way in your daily life is like asking for directions from the person who designed the map. God has a plan for you and will help you follow it, if you ask. At first, I did not know quite what to say. I started with a simple prayer from 1 Samuel in the Old

Testament: "Speak, Lord." That was it. Pretty deep, eh? As a child I had been taught that if you ask, God listens and answers. I did not know exactly what I was praying for, so I started at a basic level. As prayers go, this was probably prayer "lite"—fewer calories, less substance. As I prayed, God began to speak—through friends, sermons, books I "discovered," or a sermon that "happened" to be on the radio as I channel surfed. Only months later did I begin to think more about my simple prayer from Samuel and its context in the Bible: "Speak, Lord, for your servant is listening." I had begun to quit chattering quite so much and to listen. I felt a new sense that God was guiding me, one step, one day at a time—not monthly, but daily. The more I intentionally set aside time to focus on God, the more aware I became of God's presence the rest of the time. A relationship that had been steady became more intimate, though it took a while. It was initially sort of like stopping to get my bearings in life. I realized that once I figured out where I was going, I had to figure out how I was going to get there.

Learning How to Slow Down

How do you slow down to figure this out? You might consider starting with the prayer I mentioned: "Speak, Lord." Or: "God, please help me on my journey"; "God, please speak to me and help me hear you"; "Help me, God." Your prayer does not have to be fancy or high church. Just pull it from your heart as you seek to change your life. Perhaps when we are most desperate, God is best able to show us what is possible. At this point in my quest, the prayer was more of a desperation plea, actually. I felt like I was right back where I had started and shaky in trying to change. I think I had a destination in mind—slower, calmer, you get the picture—but I was stalled on the side of the road.

Tackle Nagging Problems

I grabbed some of my hurrying moments and turned them into transforming moments by tackling my nagging problems. Nagging problems were those issues—usually involving my schedule—that kept cropping up in my daily life. They came to symbolize the life I did not want to lead. They ranged from always running late because I left too late, or paying late charges because bills got lost in the shuffle, or putting on extra pounds because I never took time to exercise. Your nagging problems may mirror mine, or you may come up with a strong and ugly list on your own. These drain our energy and keep us from moving forward. We must deal with them—sometimes again and again—to live more fully and at a less frenzied pace.

A POSSIBILITY: Use a technique at which you are probably an expert—making lists.

Most of us have endless to-do lists, lists of cards we need to send or errands to run—not to mention the ever-present grocery list. Now is the chance to put those skills to use in learning to live more meaningfully. Take out your trusty notebook or tablet or napkin and get ready to make a rather tough list—a list of *roadblocks*. These are the circumstances, situations, or people who make it hard for you to hurry less and worry less. Consider how you wound up in this predicament in the first place. What might keep you from changing directions and slowing down your life?

In working with people who are on this journey, I hear many of the same roadblocks mentioned. They include the incredible difficulty of balancing home and work; the necessity of working to earn a living; a job that takes more time than it used to; the increasing speed of the world with more choices each and every day; an unawareness of what they really want to do with their life because they have paid so little attention to themselves for so long.

Consider your own roadblocks and how they make you feel. You need to keep your dreams in front of you, but you also need to understand what is keeping you from slowing down. List them all. Let the list pour out of you, with all the frustration that comes along with them. Begin to talk with others about your journey—starting with friends and family, colleagues, a pastor, or mentor.

You will probably get some opinions that change is not possible. Do not become discouraged if people do not provide the support for which you hoped. Again, you are going against the tide of daily life. To slow down requires a dose of courage that you will not be run over by those whizzing past you with a maniacal look in their eyes.

As I tried to change, I found that it was tough some days to stick to the path. I kept wandering off, drifting. However, the more I grew and changed, the sooner I realized when I was floundering. When you veer off the path or stumble, do not give up. Your life is meant to be lived in fullness each day, abundantly. As you become increasingly aware of that, you will correct your steps more quickly. During a time when I nearly despaired over being able to slow my life down, a friend sent me a notebook in the mail. Written on each page was the scripture from Philippians 1:6, "He which hath begun a good work in you will perform it until the day of Jesus Christ" (KJV). This verse jumped off the page and stuck in my mind. It kept coming to me, reminding me that God would continue to help change me for the better. Again and again, I felt certain that life was meant to be more than a high-speed chase. That verse became one of the tools I used to keep me moving forward.

THIS WORKS: Choose your own verse to recall. When you begin to falter, call it to mind. Write it in your notebook. Put it on the bathroom mirror.

Perhaps you have not opened a Bible in decades; maybe you do not even own one. Or, you feel like you do not have time to start something quite so "deep" as searching the Scriptures. Do not let this stop you. Consider the verse that I mentioned. Perhaps your strategies will be moved along by Jesus' words in John 10:10, "I have come that they may have life, and have it to the full." The grand plan for each person's life is this—living life to the fullest. Not worn out, fed up, surviving under the circumstances. We were meant to have abundance, goodness, and meaning in our life and work! As another of my tools, I chose inspirational quotes by people ranging from poet Emily Dickinson to German author Johann Goethe. I posted quotes on the bulletin board in the laundry room and wrote them inside my notebooks and journals—even carried them in my purse. These words from others reminded me that if I wanted to have less hurry and worry, I needed to get started.

A Journey Scrapbook

Find your own quote, or collect a basket full, to encourage you as you move forward. The wise words of others can provide reassurance when you need it most. You might also use a cut-and-paste technique to help keep you focused.

Stroll through a magazine and cut out words and pictures that speak to you of the kind of life you would like to live. Glue them into your notebook or make a journey scrapbook. While this may seem corny to some, others will find it to be a solid tool to help define what they want.

You might also dig out an old map of the United States or the world (maybe one of those in the stacks of National Geographic magazines you can't bear to throw away) or your city (if you have stayed in one place most of your life). Get a bold marker and mark your life's journey—every step of it, from birth to college to where you live now. Consider how each stop along the way is woven into you. Mark the spots where important or sad or inspiring things happened. Consider the pace of your life as you move through each spot, trying to see how it got speeded up. Think about good lessons you learned at each of the points. Consider writing some of those down.

Review Your Journey

By reflecting on our individual journeys, we see important events that have helped us get where we are and are going to provide the fuel we need to take us further. God uses what is special and unique about us to get us to the place where we should be. As you move along in your journey, you are becoming a pioneer, pushing ahead. It is not an overstatement to say you are creating something better for the world by the choices you are making. The people whose lives touch yours will be affected by your example. Perhaps one of your coworkers will decide to step back and assess his or her life. Or, one of your children will make different life decisions as a result of what you have modeled. You may even find that a friend will turn to you, inspired by your example and seeking feedback.

Making Time for Rest

DON'T FORGET: To keep at this, you will need rest.
Our harried pace wears on us physically and emotionally. Both kinds of fatigue require rest. One client with young children kept adding to her to-do list and pushing activities later and later, falling into bed at 2:00 and 3:00 A.M., only to wake at 6:00 A.M., exhausted and anxious. By planning her time around thirty minutes of "alone" time early each day and a realistic bedtime, she began to get the in-between scheduling under control. Stop routinely doing laundry well past your bedtime. Stop running tiring errands on your lunch hour and planning something for each minute of the weekend. Begin to build a day or two a week around getting a good night's sleep and then aim for more. Slow down—literally. Make yourself go the speed limit. Nearly every hurried person I have worked with admits to speeding everywhere. One man told me he skipped church one week because he felt so swamped that he needed to go to work. He had a wreck that morning, along with getting his third speeding ticket within weeks. A mom in one of my classes told me about getting stopped on her way to soccer practice with a car full of children. The policeman counseled her on slowing her life down instead of giving her a ticket.

Instead of always hurrying with your children, schedule an hour to spend *playing* with them. Most people who have young children mention this as a priority; people with older children mention it as a regret. If you must, write it on your calendar. Get down on the floor, whip out a game, watch a funny movie (with popcorn), make eye contact. Lie down on the bed and visit as you tuck them in.

Turn off the cell phone. When you get in the car, do not automatically reach for it. Instead, enjoy a minute or two of quiet. Maybe this is a good time to pray for God's help with your schedule.

Catch your breath. Many busy people have blended families, stepchildren, former spouses, and a network of complicated relationships. When the children are away for the weekend, don't decide to paint their bedroom or roof the house. Plan something fun and restful. Take a moment to catch your breath.

My mother worked hard her entire life, most of that work in food services and on her feet. When she came home each evening, she took a couple of minutes to catch her breath—usually drinking a cup of coffee and eating a slice of bread. Off came the work shoes and uniform, on went her comfortable clothes. It was a tiny unwinding ritual for her.

Find a small unwinding ritual for yourself. It does not have to be a day at a spa, but something that gives you a moment to breathe deeply and refresh your spirit.

BEGIN TO THINK: "What if I did not do this or that? What would happen?"

Skip a party you don't really want to go to. Take a vacation day in the middle of the week just to piddle around the house. Choose an activity you enjoy with your family over a work obligation that is not mandatory.

Stretching yourself too thin does not allow you any slow, patient time to enjoy the moment and savor the goodness of life. When your schedule begins to crack slightly and lets a seed like this take root, watch out! You will begin to look at your daily life with new eyes. Slowly your schedule will begin to get easier, with small changes flowing into your decisions.

When this happens, you will realize that you are on the path you want to be on, doing what you are meant to do. While there may still be twists and turns, your journey will continue to unfold with meaning and purpose.

Chapter Three

BEGIN TO BELIEVE THAT YOU HAVE ENOUGH TIME

Encouraging Word: *Time can become a friend instead of a dreaded enemy.*
Everyday Step: *Take a closer look at how you spend your time each day.*

It is very remarkable that God, who giveth plenteously to all creatures . . . yet in the distribution of time seems to be strict handed and gives it to us, not as nature gives us rivers enough to drown us, but drop by drop, minute after minute, so that we can never have two minutes together, but [God] takes away one when [God] gives us another. This should teach us to value our time, since God so values it, and by His small distribution of it tells us it is the most precious thing we have.—Bishop Jeremy Taylor

*O*ddly, in a world where so many differences exist, every human being has the same amount of time—whether we are president, plumber, pastor, waitress, writer, editor, or executive. The pope and Mother Teresa—even Jesus—had the same amount of time I have. We all have the same twenty-four hours a day, minute by minute, the same yearlong trip around the sun. Yet hardly anyone feels as if he or she has enough time. Worse, time that should be so precious and sweet has become the enemy. Even talking about time makes us nervous. It has become a four-letter word that pounds us daily.

If I had a dime for every time I had told someone I was

too busy, I'd be retired on a beach right now—and not wearing a watch! We are always trying to "make" time or "find" time, as though we are part of a cosmic scavenger hunt that will yield the treasure we say we want most. Stay up later. Get up earlier. Drive faster. Do three things at once. (Beware of the people you see each day driving too fast on their way to work, talking on their cell phones and drinking a cup of coffee and eating a granola bar.) One of the ways we get most offtrack in life is rushing around, not savoring the good things that abound. Hurry robs us of daily enjoyment and meaning.

Evaluate Your Schedule

To begin to change this rushing attitude, take a close look at what you want your day-to-day schedule to look like versus what it looks like now. This is not easy—after all, you're too busy to do this, right? You may start thinking again that you cannot slow your life down or simplify. But you can change by considering a slower pace that would not cause you to be frantic and upset, no matter how great the load.

A key strategy for slowing down is to do an audit of your time.

No one likes the word "audit," but your time audit can show you where you are wasting time, where you are misusing it, and where you need to take a closer look. We should lay out our schedules—including work and home and church and community—and examine them closely, knowing that change is possible.

Grab your notebook or a piece of paper and list how you spend your time. Think back over the past month or so and let it all pour out—time at work, housekeeping, business travel, meetings, commuting, shopping, watching television. Keep your list handy and add new activities that pop into your mind. Do not worry at this point about how much time you have spent on each activity, but try to come up with a fairly comprehensive list. Next, track your time specifically for one week—jotting down what you do and how much time you spend doing it. (For any of you who have dieted, you will immediately recognize this tool as similar to a food journal, where you keep track of how much you eat each day.) Do not obsess about your time diary, but use it as a tool to help you become more aware of what is taking up most of your time. Instead of wondering, *Where did the time go?* you can get a realistic idea. You are regaining control of your life. Perhaps you will find that even though you say you do not watch much television, you are spending an hour or more a day plopped on the couch. Or that you are chatting with coworkers longer than you thought, making your workday stretch out.

How Do You *Want* to Spend Your Time?

Once you jot down your activities, you are ready to move a step further. Assess again how you want to spend your time. Write down ways you would like to spend time—such as more time playing with the children or reading or playing golf one afternoon a week. Wander through the schedule you would like to have for your daily routine. For me, for example, this list includes a cup of coffee and journal-writing or reading time every morning, some exercise several days a week, having lunch with a friend or colleague two or three times a week, and getting home from work in time for dinner with my husband. I also like to factor in good sleep time—knowing that I feel better and get more done when I am rested.

Go ahead and dream some with your schedule. Do not be so practical that you do not include a watercolor class or a sit-down dinner with the family or visiting with a friend. This "wishful thinking" schedule will become part of your regular routine as you work on it.

Consider anew what you want your life to look like and put activities on your schedule that support that. Think about the words you chose to describe your life. For example, "tranquil" is one of my words, so I want to be certain I do not schedule an evening meeting or class or visit five or six nights a week. That is not tranquil for me. My daughter is a young working mom who longs for more time with her toddler. She makes very hard choices about time with friends on weekday evenings. Go back over your dream schedule and look at it with a slightly more realistic eye. Remember that you and everyone else in the world have twenty-four hours to spend each day—and no matter how you might try to stretch them, they will not be increased. Do not shoot down your dreams, such as learning to speak Italian for the anniversary trip you hope to take with your spouse. However, realize that you probably cannot work full-time, take Italian lessons, learn to belly dance, volunteer daily at a homeless shelter, and make balanced, home-cooked meals all at the same time.

Cut Something Out

Now, back to your real, everyday life and the schedule you kept track of for a week. What can you cut out? How can you change the way you are spending time? Most of us think we cannot cut anything out of our schedules, but we can. Anything that is not mandatory (such as a job or picking your children up at day care) can be negotiated on your calendar. And, in fact, even the time you spend at work can often be lessened. In a later chapter, we will talk about specific strategies for getting the basics of your work under control.

As you assess, for example, notice the four "quick" trips to the grocery store you made in one week. Start keeping a running grocery list on the refrigerator door and cut down on the times you must dash out to the store. Maybe you found, as one of my clients did, that you wander around the mall on your lunch hour, draining your energy and making you want to buy things you cannot afford. Or that you spent most of your reading time at the local bookstore browsing, then finding no time for reading. One client found that a walk outside at lunch helped relax her and made her schedule more manageable, so she chose to cut out regular trips to a huge wholesale warehouse store at noon. The point here is not to quit doing things you enjoy, but to make time for things you want to do.

Now that you have an idea how you want to spend your time, you can begin to shape your schedule—decision by decision—to match that. Does your family always celebrate birthdays with a Sunday supper? Do not commit to a small group meeting at church that evening. Do you want to go to a movie with your husband every Friday night? Avoid setting up a dinner gathering with friends. Do you want to be better about connecting with a network of business colleagues? Set up specific breakfast or lunch meetings with them.

Do not put something on your calendar without being certain that it suits you!

This is excruciatingly difficult at first, but it can become a habit. Years ago, as a young reporter, I was hurrying to the airport in Baton Rouge in a rental car during a rainstorm. When

I tried to slow down, I hydroplaned across two lanes and stopped inches from a concrete wall, sitting sideways across the passing lane. I still shake when I think about it. Maybe your schedule feels a lot like I did that evening—you are hurrying so fast that you cannot begin to slow down. When you try, you slide further out of control and head straight for whatever wall is staring you in the face—job advancement, caring for an aging parent, holding the household together. But you can recover without hitting that wall. Then, just as I did that evening on Interstate 10, you can slowly right yourself and head purposefully down a new road.

Time Emergency

Suppose your schedule is so out of control that you absolutely do not know where to start, but you are desperate to start somewhere. Do not take on any new commitments until you work this out—not another volunteer job or a family project or an optional work assignment. This is a time emergency, and you are simply trying to stop the bleeding by putting a tourniquet on your calendar.

Again, most of the items on our schedules are negotiable to some extent, so prepare to sit down at the bargaining table. A lot of the negotiations will be with yourself. You will be choosing what really matters. You will be deciding what needs to go. You may wind up giving up a dream or two in order to choose another dream.

In my life, I had to relinquish the piano fantasy. I had wanted since childhood to learn to play the piano. I had a warm picture of everyone gathering around the piano singing Christmas carols. I bought a piano and took a halfhearted stab at lessons. Those lasted about three months, until a big work assignment came up and I started traveling a lot, choosing my career as a journalist over my career as a concert pianist. However, I did not give up the thought that one day I would learn to play the piano, believing that a goal was a goal. That two-ton, beautiful upright piano was cursed by movers from Tennessee to Louisiana to Florida and back to Louisiana before I realized that playing the piano was just not that important to me. I had other priorities and fun things I wanted to do. I sold the piano to a woman who played the piano for a small country church. When she came to look at it, she played it in the way it should be played—and I was relieved and sad to see it go home with her. But I had one less thing to worry about fitting into my schedule, opening up time for other dreams. I had changed, and I eased a two-ton load by admitting I had other priorities.

ANOTHER STRATEGY: Occasionally choose the easy way, the cheaper way, the plainer way.

In our world, bigger is better. We are so used to trying to do more, more, more that we seldom stop to think about how to do things more easily—or whether to do them at all. One of the great gifts my laidback husband has given me is a reminder that when I start getting in a tizzy I need to "Simplify. Simplify." Those two words can stop me where I am. And on the occasions when I feel most defensive or annoyed by the reminder, he is usually most on-target. Those words are like a household railroad crossing, and they require me to stop, look both ways, and listen.

Before I cross into yet another activity, I consider whether this is really right for me and fits the way I want my life to look. I have a tendency to make things more complicated than they need to be. Perhaps you do, too. While this complicated mind-set is often reinforced by society, simplifying feels so good. It is like someone took the brick off the top of your head and you can finally relax. Simplifying your life does not mean doing nothing or becoming a sloth. It means weaving the easier way into your schedule sometimes. Go ahead and pick up dinner, instead of cooking, or postpone training for a marathon and do a 5K instead, or leave the den-painting project for another time.

Take an Activity Sabbatical

A strategy that can help manage an out-of-control schedule is the "Activity Sabbatical." This may seem extreme, but it works well for those who are so tired that they feel sick (or wish they were sick, so they could stay in bed) or for those who truly have no idea where to start.

Decide to take a sabbatical from all volunteer and extracurricular activities.

Use your calendar and a notebook or a piece of paper to sketch out a plan for this. Decide how long you need to rest or to reassess how you are living your life. Thirty days? Sixty? A summer? A full year? Then, take a break from your clubs, charitable organizations, and so forth for that time. Write a letter or make a call and explain that your schedule is out of control, and you are working to get it reorganized.

As you do this, develop a systematic way so that you can, as much as possible, keep from leaving people in a lurch. Perhaps you have a friend who wants to coach your Little League team. Or, maybe there are three coaches and two will be plenty.

During your sabbatical, you will begin to get a clear picture of what you want to do with your time and what you want to let go of. Perhaps tutoring homeless children is what you really want to do, but you have been spending your time working on an arts festival. Or, maybe you want to spend more time in your role as publicity chairman for the Rotary Club and less time coaching Little League.

As you work through this, you will likely feel guilty. But think of the stronger, more vibrant person you are going to be when your sabbatical is over. Consider the things you are doing that you just really do not want or need to be doing in the first place. The sabbatical can also be used in some work-places and can help the person who is so tired and burned out that he or she is ready to quit. Taking three months off without pay is less drastic than deciding to run away and join the circus. Allowing burned-out employees to take time off can be a big benefit for a business or organization because it can help the person come back with new ideas and enthusiasm.

Plenty of Time

Once the calendar has been tackled, start changing your language and, thus, your mind-set. Begin to get out of the habit of saying, "I don't have time" or "I'm so busy" or "I'll do that when I have the time." Instead, consider choices and answers that line up with the way you want your life to be.

Since we all have the same amount of time, we all have time to do what we need to do. Determining how to use that time is a challenge, but it is not impossible. Begin to realize that you have plenty of time to do meaningful things, and that you are more than capable of determining what is meaningful in your life and work. When you start feeling frenzied, stop. Consciously decide at that moment that you will not rush. Take a deep breath. Think, instead, "I have plenty of time." Do this until you get used to doing it. You will begin to feel a sense of relief that is almost amazing. This will gradually become part of your regular response. "I have plenty of time" is a powerful phrase and can change the way you approach each day. Always try to avoid saying, "I do not have time for that."

TRY THIS: Say no to one thing to say yes to something else.

When we say we do not have time, we are really admitting that we did not choose to use our time on that particular activity. Say no more often to things that are not important to you—or are not as important as something else. This may mean saying no to some things you would like to do or think you should do. However, when you say no to one thing, you are saying yes to other things—a concept I first read about in Claire Cloninger's book *A Place Called Simplicity* and an idea that has picked up steam in recent years in other publications.

Saying no to say yes is a most freeing way to live. To say no to an out-of-town trip with friends might be to say yes to a restful, much-needed weekend at home. To say no to a third committee assignment might be to say yes to time to cook a real supper for your family or see a long-awaited movie. And no to scrubbing the tub might be yes to a cup of coffee in the porch swing. This way of living can offer more time with your children or friends, time for projects you want to do versus ones you think you ought to do, and ways to be more of the person God wants you to be.

Seasons of Time

Another strategy is to realize that we have "Seasons of Time" in our lives—an idea I was reintroduced to by a counselor in Florida when I was considering a job change. When we understand the season we are in, we can make better decisions. There are certain times that will be crazy—but these should not be the norm. Cut yourself some slack in times of transition—relocating, getting married, getting divorced, recovering from illness, mourning the death of a parent. Many of us, even if we are not Bible readers, learned this wisdom early in life from the famous verse in Ecclesiastes: "There is a time for everything, and a season for every activity under heaven." Do not feel compelled to try to change the world on those days when you can barely comb your hair!

As you assess your Season of Time, accept the fact that as you gain things in life, there are also things you give up. My husband and I left Florida to be closer to family. We gave up a home we loved, lots of friends, and the ability to watch shuttle launches in our front yard. Now, we are lucky if we see the occasional jet fly over, but we are within a short distance from all three of my brothers and their families. We are closer to our children, and I feel a connection to the community I live in.

My good friend, who was a successful executive at a non-profit organization, is another example of someone who decided she needed to change her priorities after she became a mother. She had helped start programs that had citywide impact and threw her heart, soul, and time into her work—until she had children. After much soul-searching, she decided that her family would become her focus. In the same way that she had ministered to the community as an executive of a caring organization, she would minister to her family and equip them to go into the world.

When I was a young newspaper editor, I would often come home from work to find my next-door neighbor playing in the front yard with her three sons, the water sprinkler evoking their squeals, or a football game in progress. I would look at her and feel a twinge of envy for her playful motherhood. She would look at me and feel a twinge of envy for my professional appearance and job. We were each in a specific Season of Time. When her children were older, she went back to college and became an award-winning middle-school teacher. I later married a man with two young children and became a parent. During my early career years, I was willing to relocate frequently with my job. I was single and wanted to explore. After I married, my decisions changed.

You may give up something—a promotion or a job outside the home, for example—to be more present in your kids' lives at a certain time. Certainly the stress and demands of young children affect the day-to-day decisions and choices we make. I am reminded of something my college roommate said when her twins turned five: "We are finally mobile again." They knew they had to limit their going and doing while they were getting this new family adventure under way. You may move closer to home to care for aging and ailing parents. Or, you may retire and decide the time is right to make less money for more playtime.

Remember again the rhythm of the earth's seasons. You do not see changing leaves in winter or snow in July. One newspaper executive told me in a seminar that her preschool daughter had recently asked her to play a game. "We can do it in a hurry," the child said. The executive determined to change how she used her time. Begin to set your schedule according to the season of your life, giving yourself permission to adjust as life unfolds. When you have small children or a tough new job or a serious illness in the family, you might make different scheduling choices. Do not overbook and overdo.

A Slower Pace

Nowadays many people have their paychecks deposited directly into their accounts. The bank is always quite clear on when the money is available and how it can be withdrawn. Our use of time is much like this. There is a direct deposit—but it really is only a minute at a time. When we get going so fast that we deplete the balance too quickly, we will be overdrawn—tired, worn out, less creative. So many of life's gifts are to be savored slowly—a sunset, flowers that only bloom in the right season, children at play. We miss meaningful times in our lives because we rush right through them, roll right over them. Choose a time strategy and move forward—at a slower pace.

Chapter Four

LIGHTEN THE LOAD ON YOUR MIND

Encouraging Word: *Some worries can be discarded, the way you get rid of clothes you no longer wear.*
Everyday Step: *Set aside a worry-free week.*

Since we are always preparing for eventualities, we seldom fully trust the moment. It is no exaggeration to say that much human energy is invested in these fearful preoccupations. Our individual as well as communal lives are so deeply molded by our worries about tomorrow that today hardly can be experienced.—Henri J. M. Nouwen

*I*f worry were an art form, I would be Michelangelo. I have mastered the fine art of worrying. For years, I tried to pretend that it was genetic. My mother was a worrier. My grandmother was a worrier. "I am just worried sick," I have heard them say countless times. But somewhere along the line I noticed that my worries were not the kinds of worries Mama and Grandma had. Their worries were about things like getting into the closet when a bad storm blew through or getting stung by a wasp on a picnic. I worried about other kinds of things—how I could get my work done, how we would possibly figure out our holiday schedule, whether I would have time to get my income taxes together and clean the house before the Easter lunch. As a journalist, I spent a fair amount of time worrying that some big news story would break and make me cancel a special vacation or miss my husband's birthday dinner. I worried that someone would not be able to find me when news was breaking.

When I began to take a fresh look at my life, I realized that many of my worries went right along with hurrying. The more I hurried, the more I worried. Usually when I was hurrying, I was tired. When I was tired, I worried more. When I hurried, I could not enjoy the moment I was in because I had so much else I needed to do. So, I began to worry about all the things I had to do. This, I admit, is not a pretty picture. It bears a frightening resemblance to one of those little hamsters on a wheel. I would wake up in the middle of the night thinking about everything I needed to do. Before long, my heart would be hammering and I would be considering getting up and putting a load of clothes in the washer or answering e-mails. This, mind you, in the middle of the night.

In talking with friends, colleagues, and participants at seminars I lead, I discovered that all across the country others are lying awake too—staring at the ceiling, turning over this way, then that, fluffing the pillow, flattening the pillow, moving the pillow. During the past few years, I have been amazed by the number of people who talk about waking up in the middle of the night, worrying about what they have to do tomorrow, what they left undone today. Sometimes it seems that a dozen people are in bed with you—your boss, reminding you of another project; your parent, wanting more time with you; your child, needing direction; your best friend, wondering why you never have time for lunch anymore, and on and on.

I once saw a great piece of antiworry advice on a greeting card: "Don't put your umbrella up until it starts raining." These words have helped me immensely, reminding me that when I start fretting over something that might not even happen, I am as smart as a person standing under an umbrella just because it *could* rain.

The greeting card philosophy is backed up with something much deeper—the words of Christ in Matthew 6. Jesus reminds us not to worry and directs us to seek God's kingdom and righteousness. He tells us the things we need will be provided. Just in case we have any lingering worries, Jesus weaves in another zinger: "Who of you by worrying can add a single hour to his life?" (Matthew 6:27).

List Your Worries

To begin to worry less, it is helpful to list what you worry about. Start with about ten things, not analyzing why you worry or whether the worries are grounded in reality. Just pull out your notebook or a piece of paper and make a list of what you worry about. Most people's lists have similar items—money, their children's behavior and schoolwork, what might happen in that nebulous place called the future, their job security. I tend to worry about something happening to my husband, the safety of our children, and whether our family finances are in good order.

Go through your list and circle your top three worries. Your steps to less worry will start with these three. Consider why you worry about these and what you might do to stop worrying about them. If you see recurring themes in your worries, such as not spending enough time with your family, consider a plan for dealing with that concern. Rather than having it roll over in your stomach every day, begin to do something about it. Figure out what it will take to spend more time at home or playing with the children or helping your kids with homework or whatever is causing you to fret. Develop a plan and write it in your notebook. Try to understand what is at the root of your worries and begin to think about which ones you can throw away—or decide to worry about next month or next year. If your child is in middle school, do not start worrying about whether he or she will make good career choices. Save that concern for later.

If money is an issue, go over your finances so you have an accurate picture of where things stand. Worry often clouds the true picture and contributes to knee-jerk decisions. Try to get a clear picture: *What is coming in? What is going out? Are there areas where cuts could be made? What recurring monthly expenses might be eliminated?* From there, go a bit deeper. *How much money do you need to meet your monthly expenses and what sort of changes do you need to make to get out of debt and save appropriately?*

Just as hurry and worry go together in this discussion, time and money often go together. People want more time, but they sacrifice time because they feel they do not have enough money. They worry about providing for their children and paying their bills. Assessing what you can cut from the family budget is never pleasant but is a key part to ending money worries and to helping you find more time to slow down.

Decide what you might be willing to give up financially for less worry—and maybe the added bonus of some extra time. Do you need a new car every three to five years, or can you drive the paid-off model? Sure you could afford a bigger house, but how about staying in the smaller, cheaper, easier-to-keep-clean house? Do not automatically inflate your budget every time you get a raise or a windfall.

Expert at "Awfulizing"

You may find that you are an expert at "awfulizing"—imagining the worst that can possibly happen, taking a small problem and watching it grow. This often happens in the middle of the night, when you wake up uneasy and little voices start up in your mind. You are lying awake, thinking about how you can possibly get something done the next day; then you think about all that you have to do next week; then it escalates to how will you ever get the kids through high school and college, how you will pay all the bills, and whether there is any hope of world peace.

These midnight worries take on a life of their own, unfounded in truth but certain to make you tired and distracted come daylight. In teaching myself to worry less, I began to think of the worst thing that might happen and how I would handle that situation. When I decided to quit my very good job as a newspaper editor to open a consulting business, I worried about how my business would do, whether I would send us straight to bankruptcy or would soon be standing on a street corner promising to work for food. This "awfulizing" was curtailed by getting the facts and planning—knowing how much money I could spend in my business each month, how much I needed to take in, and so forth. Even that was not enough at first. I would wake up worrying about whether I would make enough money to keep my business going and to do my share to keep the wolf from our door. I realized that I had to quit thinking about this every day. I made a pact with myself that I would take another look at the big picture of my business finances in a few months and decide then if I needed to make changes.

As you teach yourself to worry less, pick a reassuring word—such as "trust," "peace," "joy"—or an encouraging

**passage from the Bible, and turn your mind to it when you
begin to worry.** This is especially helpful when worry-driven
insomnia kicks in. For the past few years, if I awaken and
begin to worry, instead of counting sheep, I turn to the shepherd, repeating the first verse of the Twenty-third Psalm over
and over. "The LORD is my shepherd, I shall not be in want."
This is a reminder that I have everything I need.

One summer I was considering a major career change. I
had fretted over it so much that my usually supportive
spouse was getting a bit irritated with me. So, when we went
on a vacation to celebrate our wedding anniversary, I committed not to think about my career—nor worry about it—
for the entire time. It was so restful. When I came home and
opened the can of worry again, my husband commented on
how much he appreciated the break from the "heavy"
discussions.

Another time when I was about to relocate and take a new
job, I had so many details going around in my head that I
found myself constantly worrying. The month of the move I
decided on the "No Worry" policy, no matter what happened. Instead of assuming the worst (such as thinking the
moving van would drive away with all our worldly belong-
ings and never be heard from again), I would assume the
absolute best—that the move would go well, that I would
thrive at my new job, and that our new home would be comfortable. Each of those things happened. The small things
did not grow into big things. The worry-free month helped
make the move seamless. This strategy can work anytime,
anyplace.

Set aside a worry-free week, for instance, committing not
to worry for seven whole days. If worries pop up, make a
mental note that you will worry when the week is over.
When that week ends, make a list of what is still worrying

you and discard the lowest worries on the list—whether it's that your house is too messy or that you were not invited to the boss's Christmas party. Make yourself get rid of some worries, just as you throw away worn out T-shirts or broken household items.

ANOTHER STRATEGY: When you go on vacation, leave your worries at home. Decide ahead of time not to worry.

Worries in our lives seem to grow hand in hand with busyness. Many people do not enjoy what they are doing at the moment because they are worrying about everything else they have to do. Even something fun like a special vacation becomes food for worry: How will I get everything done before I leave? How will I ever get caught up when I return?

One step to changing this is to make a decision ahead of time that you will plan for your time off and not leave too much for the last day before vacation. Consider all that will need to be done while you are gone and slice and dice it. Spread it out over the week before you leave. Delegate what might be done by someone else while you are gone, knowing that you will also help them out when they are on vacation. Consider what can be left undone. Years ago I worked with a young, ambitious manager who wanted to do everything just right. Seeing her exhausted and nearly in tears at her desk until late in the evening before she was to leave on a "restful" vacation reminded me that she needed guidance in prioritizing and handling the right details at the right time.

Pick out what must be done by you and let some of the other stuff go. When it is time for you to return to work, do not waste time dreading the stack on your desk or what might have happened while you were away. Instead, go back refreshed and ready to do your job. Take it one piece at a time. Was there a crisis while you were away? You will be able to handle it. Did something slip through the cracks? You can probably repair the damage. Not one of us is perfect, no matter how much we long to believe otherwise. When we work hard and do a good job, that is enough. We do not need to waste perfectly good brain space on worries.

Another way to meet worry head-on is to remind yourself that you can handle whatever comes your way. Consider making a list of your strengths and situations you have survived before, times you developed an inner strength that will serve you again when you need it. One of the hardest times in my life was in college when both of my parents died within two years of each other. Those were gut-wrenching, painful days when it sometimes seemed that the world would not be right again. But as each day went by, I recovered and my life began to be OK again. I made it through other traumas and dramas in my life—and know now that I can handle bad things when they arise. It is not necessary to make things worse with incessant worrying ahead of time.

Turn to God at Your Own Speed

Worry is one of the first areas in which we must learn to lean on God and ask for help. This is not easy if you have been so busy that you have not thought about God. Worriers tend to be cautious, so cautiously begin to turn your worries to God. I have found, just as the Bible promises, that when I draw near to God, my Creator draws near to me. When I am near God—praying, trying to learn more—I am less likely to worry, realizing that whatever may come my way, God will be there to help me handle it. Building this trust takes time, but it is immensely possible.

During a family crisis, a friend directed me to a passage of

Scripture that has helped end lots of worry for me and helped restore a daily bond between me and God: "Yet this I call to mind / and therefore I have hope: / Because of the LORD's great love, we are not consumed, / for his compassions never fail. / They are new every morning; / great is your faithfulness" (Lamentations 3:21-23). During the hardest days, when worries threaten to swamp you, call these words to mind. God's compassion can keep us from feeling overwhelmed. Miraculously, God's mercies are new each day, so we can start over again.

How can we live with ourselves if we waste these precious, irreplaceable moments on useless worries? And, a final thought on worrying from 1 Peter 5:7: "Cast all your anxiety on him because he cares for you." That's right, *all* of it.

Chapter Five

LISTEN FOR GUIDANCE IN A NOISY WORLD

Encouraging Word: *Help for your journey will come in unexpected ways when you start listening.*
Everyday Step: *Walk outside and observe nature.*

We live most of our life oblivious to our true identity as persons created and provided for by God. We race around as if it were all up to us to make a living. And having made a living, we believe that what we earn and what we own is what gives us identity. Life ceases to be a gift. Instead, it is something we grasp, keep, protect, and fear losing. We run to and fro—always busy and never hearing—unaware that One who is infinitely greater and loving holds our lives.
—Wendy Miller

*T*ons of information is imbedded in my brain—info that I have no idea is there. I have other stuff packed up there that can be pulled out with the right cue—even though I never really set out to learn it. For example, I can sing most of the words to the theme song from the TV sitcoms *The Beverly Hillbillies, The Brady Bunch, Greenacres,* and *Gilligan's Island.* For good measure, I can also hum the theme from *Hawaii Five-0.*

I did not learn those songs from practicing them or reading the music. I learned them from hearing them again and again. Once I start singing them, they are stuck in my mind

61

for hours. I would almost bet a copy of this book that you could launch right in on each of those songs I mentioned. Chances are you do not know merely a phrase or two—you know almost all of the words. We learn such things from repeated exposure. Sometimes we learn things that get packed away in our brains, the way we put keepsakes or Christmas decorations in boxes in the attic. When we pull them out again, we are sometimes surprised and delighted at what we find, as though we have discovered something new.

As I began to try to live my life more fully, I found some of these same principles were at work. I was pulling out things I used to know, wondering why I had packed them away in the first place. Just as I learned those songs by hearing them over and over again, I began to realize that I needed to hear advice and feedback repeatedly to move me forward. I could not hear something once and be changed from "Super Hurry Woman" to "Great Relaxed One" in a matter of hours. Repeated exposure to the ideas and thoughts I was exploring helped me absorb them. I would have to seek information and put together strategies that worked for me—from books, magazines, friends, tapes, prayer, and sermons. I learned to listen through writing in my journal, sorting ideas and thoughts, becoming more hopeful that I might slow down my life and live it the way I wanted to live it.

Learning to Listen

Throughout the quest to renew and refresh your life, you must constantly recall where you are headed, what is important to you, and what you want your life to be like. You will also need to develop your ability to listen in a very noisy world—to begin to discern messages that can help you make good decisions in your life each day.

Learning to become a better listener includes learning to hear God's voice—again or for the first time—and learning to pray about each step you take. This may not be easy. As our lives become more harried, we often lose whatever connection we had with God—whether that was a deep heritage of faith or never more than a passing thought. We must step away from the noise and distractions, or we may miss what God has to say. We seem to think we have to be terribly holy or that there is some magic way to learn to hear God. A big part of it is listening and learning a better way to live along the way—just the way we listened to those songs and learned them without meaning to. The more determined I became to live abundantly, the more I realized that I would *have* to have God's help. As the weeks and months went by, I knew that God wanted me to quit being in a tizzy all the time, that the Bible outlined the way I was to live, and none of that included hurrying through every day, worn out and worried. I began to learn to recognize God's voice—and, thus, know more clearly what I needed to do. The more I listened for that voice, the more I learned to recognize it. Once I recognized it, it began to stay with me through the day.

You do not have to be a biblical scholar to hear God's promises and cling to them. You do not have to have a theology degree to discern what the Lord is saying. God speaks to each of us in very personal ways, in ways similar to those a dear friend or beloved relative speaks to us. To hear the conversations of others, we know we must often turn the television down, switch off our cell phones, or move to a quieter spot. The same is true of hearing from God.

A great passage in the Bible describes how God may not

talk to us in a roar of wind or a loud voice. In 1 Kings 19:11-13, the story is told:

> The LORD said, "Go out and stand on the mountain in the presence of the LORD, for the LORD is about to pass by."
> Then a great and powerful wind tore the mountains apart and shattered the rocks before the LORD, but the LORD was not in the wind. After the wind there was an earthquake, but the LORD was not in the earthquake. After the earthquake came a fire, but the LORD was not in the fire. And after the fire came a *gentle whisper.* When Elijah heard it, he pulled his cloak over his face and went out and stood at the mouth of the cave.
> Then a voice said to him, "What are you doing here, Elijah?" (italics added)

Just as in this story, God is quite likely to choose to speak to us in a whisper—even though we live in a world of wind and earthquakes and fire.

For more than two decades I worked in a newsroom and was surrounded by noise—telephones, multiple televisions, dozens of simultaneous conversations, printers, police radios, and a pneumatic tube that carried page proofs from the composing room to the newsroom, depositing them with a rather loud thud. In addition, for many of those years, my office was located in a part of the building only a few feet away from a major intersection, with plenty of traffic noise and screeching tires, sometimes followed by ugly crunches. My workplace was noisy. But I learned to shut out the noise that did not involve me directly, and got to the point where I did not notice traffic noises or the regular squawk of the police radio. And when I got in my car or first got home from work, I wanted peace and quiet—no radio, no TV. I discovered that the process of trying to figure out who to listen to as I made my way to a more abundant life required many of the same strategies. I had to learn what to ignore, what to hear, and when to allow some time for quiet. As I did that, I began to be more aware of messages that seemed to be coming at me from a variety of directions.

One of the first strategies if we are to hear is to eliminate regularly some of the noise in our lives. To do that, we must decide that there are times when we will not have the television or radio on, but be in silence. Or, we will turn off our cell phone at certain times—including in the car, at restaurants, and when we have a few minutes alone. Instead of immediately dialing a friend, we will contemplate what is going on in our lives and how we are trying to live. Instead of automatically turning on the radio, we will allow our brains to listen to ideas and possibilities. God is powerful and the Creator of all, not limited in ways to speak to us in a noisy world. Perhaps God will use an answer to your prayers or a Scripture passage or something you hear in a sermon or lesson at church to communicate with you. Perhaps God will speak through nature, or friends and family, or books, or music. The Holy Spirit might use any of these to help you get your life where it was meant to be. As you begin to pay more attention to hearing, God will speak to you in myriad ways.

Perhaps one of the easiest strategies to get you started listening is to step outside and let nature help you. My friend has a cabin at the Palo Duro Canyon in the panhandle of Texas. She told me once that she learned more about life from watching nature there than she did in most other ways. When I was hurrying all the time, I seldom noticed nature. When I started to slow down, I realized that it was a constant reminder of how life should be lived. Nature does not hurry. It is certain. The bare trees on my jogging path will bud beautifully in the spring. A few weeks later the wisteria will bloom and smell so good I can hardly stand it. The summer green will be deep and full. The leaves will be bright and slowly die and drift down on me as I run in the fall. It is so basic, but it reminds me of how there is, indeed, a time for everything in my own life. In winter, I can hunker down and work on my goals a bit more. I look at the year past and what worked and what did not. I set priorities for the year ahead, remembering that I cannot do everything. In spring, I begin to look for signs that those seeds planted earlier are sprouting and to think of what I need to do to make sure they bloom. I clean out some of the junk in my life (and my house) to make way for new things to grow. Summer is a time for fun and living with a bit more abandon, a time I try to relax even more. When I falter, I recall those days as a child on Samford Avenue when ten kids gathered in our yard to play "kick the can" at twilight, squealing and laughing and making wild attempts to grab fireflies. Come fall, I find myself becoming a bit more introspective and considering changes I want to make.

To use nature as a tool, do a "walkabout" in your own yard, strolling slowly, noticing trees, plants, birds. Take the children to the park and notice the world while they play. Go to a local lake and sit and observe your surroundings. Go on a picnic. Invest in a porch swing and sit and watch. Put up a bird feeder and notice which birds come when and how they interact.

Appreciate beauty. Begin to be aware of the seasons and how symbolic they are in your life. The beginning of each season offers a great time for a new start, for assessing where we are in our lives and where we want to be. We can understand growth better, how life ebbs and flows.

Another key to listening in a noisy world is to set aside a

few minutes for meditation or prayer each morning. Most people find setting aside time for prayer and meditation amazingly helpful in keeping them on track to living more abundantly. I have found this to be true in my own life, although it is a difficult strategy to begin. The urge to sleep late, the need to get up and exercise, getting children ready for school and early business meetings all conspire to keep it from happening. Do not be discouraged if you cannot do this every single day. Begin to do it a couple of days a week, add a couple more, and before long you will have a regular habit.

As part of this quiet time, consider adding some reading time—or set aside a bit of time before sleep to read. Get a devotional book that you enjoy and read from it or read the Psalms or an inspirational book that you feel will help you grow. Reading does not have to be an hour session. Snatch a moment or two at first, and you can add time as your life falls into place. You might also stick a book in your briefcase or purse and pull it out when you are waiting for your car to be washed or are stuck in a traffic jam.

While listening for guidance on your journey, turn to the Bible. Again, you do not have to be a biblical scholar or be able to find every book in the Bible in record time. Many Bible study books are available, and you might choose one from a bookstore shelf based on a topic you want to work on. Or, you might ask your pastor or a friend who reads the Bible to recommend a book of the Bible to peek into. Trying to read the Bible more these past few years, I have been encouraged anew by the richness of the material there. God has spoken to me dozens of times through a verse or story.

Get a View from the Pew

Consider becoming involved in a church, starting with your basic worship attendance and branching out in areas that work for you. When I got superbusy in my career, I began to find Sunday mornings a great time to sleep in, get caught up on chores, and to rest. My church attendance would not have earned a gold star. Most of us—no matter how organized and together we are—still find that we have more to do than we can get done. I found it necessary to commit myself to attending church each week, unless I was truly sick or out of town. Attending church regularly has exposed me steadily to God's word through sermons and music. When I am struggling with changes in life or looking for a better way, it often seems as though the message is aimed straight at me. That has happened again and again during this journey. I have no doubt that one way God speaks in my noisy world is through church.

If you have not been to church in a while, try a simple prayer to help you get started. Ask God to lead you to a church where you can learn new strategies for living abundantly.

Ask around at work or in your neighborhood, or look in the newspaper or Yellow Pages for services and find one that seems right. Pray again and visit to see if it is a place where you can begin to be transformed. If not, try another. This process can be discouraging because it sometimes feels like you are shopping for a church. Do not give up hope, nor be too critical. Remember, you are trying to find ways to live more fully. Most church services will offer at least a nugget for you. You will find the right place for you if you are committed to this.

From the worship service, step into the life of the church

a bit deeper, picking a group or class to attend. You will be astounded as you begin to grow and to learn more about being the person you want to be—and the one God called you to be. Many churches have small groups now, composed of a few folks who gather to discuss a study book or the Bible and share joys and concerns. On my journey, a small group of working women at a church in Melbourne, Florida, became teachers, friends, and mentors for me; and helped me grow. Again, connecting with a new group sometimes feels awkward, but look at this as a necessary step to make your life what you want it to be. The first time I met this group, I did not know anyone. I felt a bit out of place and shy and considered not going back. But that changed as I got to know them and they got to know me. Though different in many ways, we were remarkably similar in our hope of being transformed in our daily lives. We only met twice a month, often choosing a book of the Bible to read and discuss. From those meetings, I was reacquainted with the book of James, a great book to read for people who are leaders or people like me who tend to have trouble holding their tongues. From James 1:2-6 comes the wonderful reminder about how hard times can help us grow:

> Consider it pure joy, my brothers, whenever you face trials of many kinds, because you know that the testing of your faith develops perseverance. Perseverance must finish its work so that you may be mature and complete, not lacking anything. If any of you lacks wisdom, he should ask God, who gives generously to all without finding fault, and it will be given to him. But when he asks, he must believe and not doubt, because he who doubts is like a wave of the sea, blown and tossed by the wind.

And, a few lines further, in verse 17: "Every good and

perfect gift is from above, coming down from the Father of the heavenly lights, who does not change like shifting shadows." These words were so reassuring to me—reminding me that I needed to be steadfast on my journey and that God would provide wisdom and was solid and not shifty. Most mornings as I walk in to work, I ask God for wisdom for whatever challenges the day may bring. As a newspaper editor, I needed this guidance in my work in the community. As a business owner, I need it to be certain I am continuing to follow God's will about how I use my time. And, a good final reminder from James is that we should "be quick to listen" as we consider changing in our noisy world.

Once you begin to get reacquainted with the Bible, you can choose some verses as your own—guides that help you make it through the day and that encourage you as you change. For example, I find the alarm clock to be a most annoying invention and often wake up, well, cranky. So, I began to say Psalm 118:24 as soon as I woke up: "This is the day the LORD has made; / let us rejoice and be glad in it." My wake-up attitude changed and my day got off to a better start. When I was particularly exhausted, I would turn to Isaiah 40:28-31, a passage I was first introduced to at 7th & James Baptist Church while a student at Baylor University in the mid 1970s:

> Do you not know?
>   Have you not heard?
> The LORD is the everlasting God,
>   the Creator of the ends of the earth.
> He will not grow tried or weary,
>   and his understanding no one can fathom.
> He gives strength to the weary
>   and increases the power of the weak.

Even youths grow tired and weary,
    and young men stumble and fall;
but those who hope in the LORD
    will renew their strength.
They will soar on wings like eagles;
    they will run and not grow weary,
    they will walk and not be faint.

My goodness—those words can speak to us every day in a hurried world.

Worried? Choose a verse that helps you wake up reassured. Sad? Choose a verse of encouragement. God will certainly begin to speak to you through these verses. Somehow the more we recall them, the more we hear from God through them—and in deeper, unique ways that suit us wherever we happen to be at that moment.

Another strategy is to write a verse and carry it in your wallet. For years, I carried a copy of the verses from Philippians 4:4-7, until it was falling apart. It constantly reminded me of the person I was trying to become and of God's love for me. "Rejoice in the Lord always, I will say it again: Rejoice! Let your gentleness be evident to all. The Lord is near. Do not be anxious about anything, but in everything, by prayer and petition, with thanksgiving, present your requests to God. And the peace of God, which transcends all understanding, will guard your hearts and minds in Christ Jesus." Words from that passage would pop into my mind in a difficult work situation (be gentle) or when I was upset (God's peace is available even when things are not going well).

Post a verse around the house—on the refrigerator door, for example. Before long, these verses begin to pop into your mind and help you as you make calmer decisions each day.

Look to Books

In addition to the Bible, I found guidance in many other books. I have always loved books and enjoyed reading, but certain books began to appear on my path as stepping stones to get me where I wanted to be. A friend would mention a book that seemed perfect to help answer a question I had been considering. My pastor would hand me a book and say, "I thought you might be interested in this." That book would strike me right in the heart. A colleague at work would come into my office and tell me about a book she had really enjoyed and give me a copy. A reading list in a class at church would contain a book that had so much helpful information that it seemed to have been written for me. As an example, at a very painful part of my journey, my pastor in Florida mentioned a book called *Synchronicity: The Inner Path of Leadership* by Joseph Jaworski. I could not read that book quickly enough. Jaworski was writing in a deep and thoughtful way about the ability to shape our future with a focus on leadership. He introduced me to one of my favorite journey concepts: "predictable miracles," wonderful things that unfold as we begin to take steps to change.

At the end of this book, I have included a list of some of these books with the hope that they will help you on your journey. The ideas I picked up for them are woven through my life and, thus, through this book. You may come up with your own list, but perhaps some of these will speak to you.

A KEY STRATEGY: Be open to reading a wide variety of books that will help you find ways to hurry less, worry less.

Start keeping an ear to the ground to pick up on books that might help you and jot them down in your notebook. Start looking for ways to spend time reading each week. Again, you do not have to carve out hours. Begin to take a book in the car with you to read during found moments. Use your lunch hour to read for a while. Read with a highlighter or pencil in hand and underline sentences that speak to you. Write notes in the margins. I use a mechanical pencil and have developed my own book code that helps me get back to important passages when I pick the book up again. A few years back I started writing in a book's front when I bought it and when I read it. I started writing the date in the margins when a passage really spoke to me. Then, when I pick up the book again, I am reminded of my journey—how far I have come and changes I have yet to make. I also do this in my Bible when I jot notes from a sermon or when something speaks to me in a particularly compelling way.

Some books will not do much for you at the moment, but they may become dear to you later on. Others will sit on your shelf unread until they catch your eye. You pull them down and they offer you something you needed that day. An example of this for me was John Ortberg's book *If You Want to Walk on Water, You've Got to Get Out of the Boat.* I bought this book months before I got around to reading it. When I did, I was in the middle of making a gut-wrenching decision, trying to discern whether I needed to leave my work as a journalist and start my own business. Ortberg's book was perfect for me at that time and offered many good tips for my journey.

Some books become words you turn to for different insights at different times. In 1989, a coworker at the newspaper gave me a copy of *My Utmost for His Highest,* the classic devotional book by Oswald Chambers, as a going-away gift. I tried to read it and found it hard to understand. A few years later, I picked it up again and wanted to devour it. Every page seemed to have a message just for me. It led me to new verses in the Bible. It overwhelmed me with its wisdom. Now I consider it one of the staples of my personal book collection, one of those books I would like to have on a desert island.

Magazines also became helpful resources as I learned to live more fully. Certainly, they were not quite as daunting as some of the books that came my way. I could easily carry them on airplanes or to lunch. I began to search for specific magazines that seemed to encourage and help me to think differently about my life. I tore out articles that had nuggets of information that I wanted to think about. I tried out new magazines that I had not known about. A friend told me about a magazine she had discovered called *Discipleship Journal.* When I picked up a copy, it contained lots of good articles to help me. I also found Oprah's new magazine to be quite useful because its theme was "live your best life"— exactly what I wanted to do.

I found, sadly, that I often got so busy that the magazines stacked up. But one of my strategies became squirreling away some time on a weekend when I would plow through those magazines and tear out articles that spoke to me. I will admit that sometimes I attacked this, instead of doing it at a leisurely pace, but I nearly always wound up feeling refreshed, nonetheless. I sometimes even cut out headlines or photos and put them in my notebook to remind me of a goal or dream for my own life.

Set Aside Time

Pick a time each day you will begin to think of God— whether it is when you wake up or when you are showering or when you are driving to work. Get in the habit of asking God to speak to you during this time. Be on the lookout for other ways that God guides you. Expose yourself to God's word through reading your Bible or attending church or finding a small group that will guide you. Read and soak up the words of others. Wander through your yard. "Speak, Lord, for your servant is listening."

Chapter Six

FIGHT FEAR

Encouraging Word: *You can figure out exactly what to do and when.*
Everyday Step: *Practice waiting calmly.*

I don't know what God has in store for me, but I feel so serene that it doesn't matter. What do I have to be afraid of when I'm with Him?—Brother Lawrence

*M*ost people get on an airplane with trust in the pilot and the equipment. While there may be a white knuckle or two, passengers know that when the plane goes into the clouds, radar takes over and the plane continues on course. Even when the ground is indistinguishable and vision totally blocked, the pilot is calm and sure. The passengers are not yelling at or pleading with the pilot, telling him or her to hurry up. We wait for the pilot to do what he or she knows how to do, and we land safely. Many times I have wished trust were that easy in everyday life. For some reason, we find ourselves predisposed not to trust that things will work out right. Instead, we lean toward believing that, in fact, anything that can go wrong will. Getting past this negative thinking and trusting that things will work out in marvelous ways is an intriguing part of the journey to less hurry and worry.

As you start trying to change your life, certain fears begin to weave themselves into your thoughts and actions—fear about the future, about how to sustain the progress you have made, and about whether you are indeed on the right path. You are forced to face hard issues such as how much money you are willing to trade for time, whether you are doing the right things as a parent, and whether you are in the right career.

Searching for Easy Answers to Hard Questions

As I wrestled with these particular worries, I wanted easy answers to hard questions. I did not want to wait for the right answers to unfold; I wanted them immediately. I wanted to look out the plane's window and clearly see where I needed to land. In the same way that I rushed through life, I wanted to rush through changing my life for the better. I found that it cannot be done like that. The journey to living abundantly has to be done more deliberately. Otherwise, it would be like my efforts to learn French from a tape in the car—I knew a few words for a few days. I had spent my life reading books such as *The Incredibly Lazy Person's Guide to a Much Better Body in 30 Days* and *Less Stress in 30 Days*. I wanted instant change. However, what instant potatoes are to real potatoes is what instant change is to meaningful change. Deep, lasting, transforming change would not come by "just adding water." It would take time and trust, and that was something *else* I needed to work on.

This stage of the journey is a bit like the discovery process in a court case. You are gathering information, fact-finding, sifting through evidence for clues about how you truly want to live and waiting to hear the verdict after the information has been presented. This waiting strategy allows an opportunity to consider more closely what you are willing to give up to gain something else. It is a time for realizing that you cannot, in fact, do everything, but you can do plenty and do it well and happily. For me, it was the time when I came face-to-face with how impatient I am and how much I need patience to live abundantly. My thinking was often all or nothing—the awful scenario, the miraculous scenario. Reality was usually somewhere in the middle. I had to learn to steer my thoughts to the right place. Having decided to change, I wanted to rush forward. The people I coach often do the same thing. If they are at a career crossroads, they want to bail immediately or grab the first job that comes along, even if it in no way matches their goals. They flirt with pursuing their dreams and then want to take a sure thing rather than wait.

Make a Timeline

A good step to take here is to make a timeline, a very useful tool for staying on course and helping you do the right thing at the right time. In your notebook, jot down some of the steps you need to take as you decide where your efforts might take you. This could include basic steps, such as getting a library card and checking out books that offer encouraging information. It might include setting up a lunch appointment to ask for advice from a friend. When I began to consider opening a business, I met with several people who have their own business for their feedback. If you want to exercise more, you might put a 5K race on your timeline. Are you feeling burned out and worn out? Find a retreat and start planning to attend it. The timeline becomes a plan, and most of us need a plan of some sort. By jotting down your ideas, you can plot and plod, instead of trying to leap through hoops, winding up exhausted and overdoing it.

The timeline can keep you from doing something rash without thinking it through appropriately. You decide upon a period of time that you will gather information and wait. You do not make a major change unless an emergency occurs. For example, a client was having a lot of trouble juggling work and home and felt that she was not doing what she was supposed to do. She was ready to bail right out of work without a parachute and without determining how hard the landing would be. By slowing down her actions and deciding to seek the best path, she took time to gather accurate information. Her family finances would not allow her to make such a change at that time. She was not ready to go to a less satisfying job. She would continue on her path, reading, journaling, and praying until she knew for sure what to do. After a few months, she was more rested, encouraged, and certain she knew what to do.

Record Your Accomplishments

Another strategy is to keep a list of things you have done to begin to live with less hurry and worry, to live to the fullest. Most people tend to overlook what they have accomplished and focus instead on what still needs to be done. When you take an inventory, you will be amazed by the books you have read or people you have spoken to or small changes you have made in your daily routine. This strategy can keep you reminded that even when you feel like you are running in place, you are actually moving forward. It can also keep you from grabbing the wrong thing just to make sure you have something to hold on to. While you are at it, list the little miracles that have come about since you decided to give living a fuller life a try. Each time I do this, I am astounded. Good things pop up along the way.

Let Things Unfold in Their Own Time

A few years back, I took a leave of absence from my job as a newspaper editor and began to explore other possibilities for my life. Almost as soon as I left the newspaper, other editing positions began to arise. I worried that I should grab one immediately, even though I was not looking for an editorial job at that moment. It was so hard to wait, but when I did, it worked out right every time.

But how do you to learn to wait? I struggled with this as much as any other part of trying to live more fully. If everything did not fall into place on my journey, despite my best efforts, I would become convinced that what I was moving toward was unattainable. Bad days blindsided me. If I had a day when I was rushed or when I tried to do something differently or pursue a dream or fun idea and it went belly up, I panicked. Happiness and thankfulness would fight a war with the feeling that something was missing, that things were not lined up quite right. I would try to force things to work that clearly were not meant to be. This required more new strategies in my life.

When things are not working, despite all manner of finagling, step back. See what happens. This is akin to making bread and seeing if the dough is going to rise. One of the good things about learning patience is learning to appreciate each day, no matter how frazzled we feel. I receive a daily e-mail prayer from a pastor in South Louisiana. One of his recent daily prayers ended by asking God to "let today's adventure begin." This struck me as the approach many of us want to take each day on the journey to living more abundantly, treating each day as part of a bigger picture and today's adventure as part of our story. It takes each day's adventures to mold us into the people we need and want to be and to help us understand what we are to do next.

About now you must also learn to realize that certain days are just not that great—adventure or not. That does not mean you are all mixed up or that things will never be right again. It means that you need to learn to deal with the bad days and move on. I was reminded of this with hurricane force one day recently. The heat went out at home, and the entire unit needed replacing—at what seemed like an exorbitant cost. The weatherman predicted a high of 57, but it only got to 42. Local department stores were sold out of electric heaters. Those heaters, they told me, were "seasonal," so none would be forthcoming. My husband was home sick with strep throat and perhaps just a little bit grumpy. The links on my business Web site were not working—pointed out nicely to me by a major client I was trying to woo. I included an error in my e-mail response to her, noticing it soon after hitting the send button. That day resurrected doubts the likes of which I had not known in weeks. I am embarrassed to admit that I sat at my desk and cried, wondering if I was way off course in my life. Then I thought back over all the steps that had brought me to this time and this place and remembered that this was one bad day. The next day would be better. Some days are like that, no matter where you are.

This does not mean that you are hopelessly offtrack or incapable of living life to the fullest. Such days serve as important reminders that I need to be very careful about acting like I have all the answers and like life all fits together with no trouble. It is a process, and I sometimes thrash about. Days like this may help each of us emerge, though, more certain than ever that we can do all things through Christ who strengthens us—ordinary us—on our everyday journeys.

In one of the most tumultuous times of change for me, I wrote in my journal: "I like change and activity, and I have been thrilled with these past months of my journey—but I continue to learn and grow and realize that Great Change is a process with many steps. And the next step I crave is a calmer life yet, more centered on one place, more connected." I was several years into this and still a long way from being just who I thought I wanted to be. I wondered how some days could be filled with searing uncertainty, while other days felt so sure, how my heart could feel so raw one day and so peaceful the next. It would take more time. Even at this point, I felt that activities and busyness were like kudzu, the Southern vine that covers up everything in sight, threatening to choke out life. Here, however, I also began to realize that this journey into becoming what I am called to be flows just as life does. Some days the river is clear and swift; other days it is murky and filled with debris. Along the way I came to depend upon signs and symbols of change— the budding peach tree that had been so stark the day before, a gorgeous sunset saying farewell to a tough day, a verse of Scripture on a church billboard. Such signs can help us learn to wait with hope.

Despite the occasional bad day and the days when I wanted to force things, I also found an increasing number of days of absolute certainty—that I was making good decisions, that I was on a journey and just passing through certain situations. I began to feel the need in my life to be useful and to serve. I had moments when I felt an odd combination of peacefulness and excitement, knowing I was that day doing what I needed to do and that great things would continue to unfold. The cadence of my life was beginning to feel right.

The strategy that helped this happen was to keep walking forward, one day at a time, focusing on what my priorities were and making good choices.

This meant turning to God, remembering each day that the Lord of All has a plan for me. It meant not being seduced into making decisions without thought and prayer. This hit me in an almost eerie way one morning as I was out jogging and praying that I would know what to do. That morning, I heard an answer to my prayers, as clearly as if God had spoken aloud. "Do you trust me?" God asked. "Well, sure," I thought, almost impatiently. "Then trust me," was the reply. When I have faltered or found myself flailing since then, I remember that. How odd—trust means trust. All these strategies have led me to a place where I am to be, although not necessarily where I will land for good. God is to be trusted and wants me to slow down. God wants me to succeed with God's plan.

Chapter Seven

LEARN TO MAKE THIS WORK AT WORK

Encouraging Word: *Basic strategies can help you regain control over your work schedule.*
Everyday Step: *Keep a good, organized calendar.*

*Better one hand with tranquility
than two handfuls with toil
and chasing after the wind.*—Ecclesiastes 4:6

*S*everal years ago, this e-mail from a college student made the rounds:

Dear Mom & Dad,
I have so much to tell you. Because of the fire set off by the student riots, I experienced temporary lung damage and had to go to the hospital. While I was there, I fell in love with an orderly, and we have moved in together. I dropped out of school when I found out I was pregnant. He got fired because of his drinking, so we're going to move to Alaska, where we might get married after the birth of the baby.
Signed, Your loving daughter.
P.S. None of that really happened, but I did flunk my chemistry class and I wanted you to keep that in perspective.

Enjoying life nearly always involves our perspective on work—how we see our jobs, how we react to our tasks and coworkers, what we want our nine-to-five life to be like, and what we are willing to do to make that so. On my own journey, I had to confront this again and again.

Our good intentions about changing our way of life sometimes get stalled at the office. Many folks cannot take the first step because they believe their bosses keep them from practicing a balanced life. Perhaps you have taken a rare day off or a vacation and find yourself dreading going back. You suspect when you walk into the office on Monday, that it will be horrible with a capital H.

Much of our overload comes with how we *feel* about the work we are doing and how that fits in our lives. We are more content in our work—and our overall days—when we are plugged into the right spot. This means doing work that suits our gifts, our personalities, our idea of what we want our lives to look like. Discovering what that work is may be easier when we slow down and consider what we enjoy about our jobs and what bugs us. Make a list of what drains you at work and begin to consider how to change those things. List what you like about work, acknowledging that there are likely many advantages to being where you are.

Change One Thought at a Time

Begin to change your negative thinking about work—one thought at a time. Take a deep breath. Begin to react differently. Your perspective will change.

NEXT STEP: Regain control of your life—whoever you are, whatever you do—by learning how to improve your work situation or by considering other options. Endless complaining only drains you and will not help you in your efforts to be calmer and more fulfilled.

You may discover you are in the wrong job. Or, you may find you are right where you need to be. Many people have demanding jobs that take lots of time and energy—and nearly every job has its own kind of stress. Consider the air-conditioning repairman who must crawl through hot attics in summertime, the secretary who fields the angry calls of dissatisfied customers, the teacher who has to hold together classes of children needing immense time and attention.

Most folks have days when they think their job is the hardest, most stressful, and absolutely worst. However, every day should not seem horrible, and we should not resent going to work each day, dislike our colleagues, and hope we can hang on until retirement.

The key is often in how we approach tough jobs. We need to feel that the work we are doing—whatever it is—matters. We need to be using the special gifts and talents we have. While we may not leap out of bed on Monday mornings, we need to enjoy our work and be thankful for it. And if we cannot abide the work we do, we must consider changing jobs, even if it means making less money.

Think about where you are right now stresswise in your work. Pull out your notebook and rate your stress level or mark on the line below. Number one represents hardly any stress; you're lying in a hammock (on a vacation you received because you did such a great job on a project), reading a good book with a cold drink in hand, and the children are at Grandma's for the week. Number ten indicates extremely high stress: you are due for a corporate onsite visit at your plant, a disgruntled employee needs to see you immediately, your temporary dental crown fell off and you swallowed it, and the school called to say your teen did not show up for class.

1 _____ 10
(Not Much Hurry and Worry)   (Lots of Hurry and Worry)

After you get a reading on how you feel about work, you must start thinking about why you feel that way and how to change your perspective, how to move further from the ten and closer to the one. Think of ways it might work—baby steps, if you will, little changes you might make to get the balance you need and want.

Many people feel paralyzed when they stop to assess where they are. Our first reaction is often that we have little control over work. We have built up habits over the years and are blind to possible new ways of doing things at our old jobs. If you are unhappy or worn out from work, it is especially critical that you try to develop new, more fulfilling habits.

An executive client struggled for years with working too late. She seldom got home for dinner with her husband and evenings were spent collapsed on the sofa, worrying about all she had to do, but not doing anything. Somewhat reluctantly, she set a goal to leave on time at least two nights a week. She was ecstatic when she made it home in time to cook dinner, one of her pleasures in life. Getting home earlier left her with more energy to tackle some household projects she wanted to handle. And at work? She found she was getting more done in less time because she felt refreshed each day. She gradually increased her goal to getting home on time every night unless there was a work emergency.

Whatever work you do, remember Proverbs 16:3, "Commit to the LORD whatever you do, / and your plans will succeed." I suspect that God does not find us committed when we are miserable in our work and spend hours doing something that is a grind. Nearly all of us can do some things differently. And some of those steps will make us better employees, wasting less time and energy on the job.

Slow Down for Better Decisions

Often we rush to make decisions. When we slow down, we can see more clearly. We help people who work for us become better at what they do. Our families prosper when the fuzziness of rushing gives way to more clarity at a slower pace. Many businesses concentrate on the ROI in daily work—"return on investment." By learning to live with more meaning, the return on our investments—personally and professionally—can be great.

A colleague who works with computers and information services for a large business found herself working constantly, in the office or on call, from her computer at home or from her laptop on the road. She was worried about her staff and knew she was not spending enough time with her family. She longed for a minute or two each day just to take a walk with her dog. Very deliberately, she decided to try to change, admitting that she did not know if it was possible.

She began to plan her work schedule better and to look for ways to be more effective at the office. She explained projects and deadlines more clearly to her coworkers and let them do their jobs, instead of trying to micromanage. She decided to go to a yoga class at least once a week. She became more committed to getting home in time for dinner. Slowly, she came to see that she was a much better leader, spouse, and mom when she slowed down. And, she found that when she did slide back into her overwhelmed ways, she was able to bounce back more quickly.

Personal and Professional, One and the Same

Some people do exciting and challenging work. Others do more routine jobs. But no matter what the role, work can

89

take a mighty toll, especially when it gets out of whack with the rest of your life. Business is demanding—whether you are a plumber's helper or the CEO of a company. The economy fluctuates, the stock market ebbs and flows, customers demand more and more.

Lots of demands converge to make work life difficult, and this convergence collides with our personal lives. As a young manager, I believed that people could separate their personal and professional selves, leaving home behind when they walked through the office door. Years later I realized that employees do not leave problems at home—their divorces or ailing parents or problem teens or bounced checks come right in, too. Work and home are connected.

If you implement strategies for improvement in one area of your life, the other area will often be helped. Many people have chosen—or been called—to tough careers. Plain old hard work. Sometimes you truly are doing all that you can do. You have to know when to step back, take a break, do things differently.

Perhaps you are tired. Your career seems to be going great on the surface, but you dread going to work every day. Even the message light on your answering machine stresses you out.

After deciding what your stress level is, think for a few moments about what causes you stress and fatigue and what gives you energy. This, again, is often unique to each person. Grab your notebook and write down the things that cause you stress at work and in your personal life. Capture those things that jump immediately into your mind, the ones that can cause your head to feel like it might just be ready to explode.

TRY THIS: Think about what *might* work for you, little steps you can take today—*not* when you retire, when business eases up, or the economy improves.

Tools for Getting Your Work Under Control

Certain strategies will make a huge positive difference in your life—if you are willing to try them. First, get the basics of your work under control. This is, at its most fundamental level, sort of like housetraining a puppy. If you do not do that pretty quickly and thoroughly, there will be lots of messy cleanup projects. It took me much too long to realize that I could control a lot of things at work—things I had let control me for much too long.

Two simple tools help get work organized—one is a calendar, the other is a notebook to keep a running list of things you want or need to do. (If you are high tech, you might use a personal handheld computer.) Ahh, the calendar—I am amazed at how many smart people do not use their calendars effectively. If you put every meeting and appointment on your calendar as soon as you know about it, you will save yourself much grief. Put all meetings on your calendar as soon as you learn of them—even if they are still tentative. (Are you available for a staff retreat on June 20? Write it down. Then, if it comes through, you haven't scheduled something over it. If it does not, you have some open time.) Write down dental appointments, your daughter's recital, other personal obligations. This keeps you from planning a work appointment over an important personal commitment. Get the special occasions in your life—anniversaries, birthdays—on your calendar. Many events at work can be scheduled flexibly. By knowing when you have personal plans, you can often avoid conflicts.

Another easy way to reduce stress and help lighten the load at work is to have one place where you jot things down—to-do items, people you need to follow up with, phone calls you need to return. This can prevent that feeling you get when you are tearing up your desk looking for a scrap of paper you wrote a note on, scrambling through your pockets, purse, briefcase and, finally, trashcan. I use a spiral journal-type notebook, although a handheld computer or fancy planner will work, too. I nearly always have this with me at work—for every meeting and at my desk. I jot down thoughts that run through my mind that I need or want to follow up on. I also write down things I have delegated that I want to touch base on. This keeps me focused; priorities rise to the top. This does not become an overwhelming daily to-do list, but lessens stress because I do not worry about forgetting something. It has made me a much more effective leader, both in my newsroom days and in my consulting work.

The next strategy: Remember you cannot do it all.

If you believe that you can be the head of a major company, make beautifully decorated cookies for each holiday, write the great American novel, sew your children's Halloween costumes, raise show horses, and grow a garden all in the same year, you are in for a lot of frustration. Look back at your list of words that describe your ideal life, and make decisions that suit that list. Maybe a plain-old cookie or store-bought costume will do. Maybe the novel will stay in your head for a while yet.

Set Some Boundaries at Work

One of the hardest things about being a dedicated worker is the feeling that you are somehow always on call, that you have to take work home with you (if not physically, then in your mind where you stew over it all evening). Boundaries with work are not easily established.

Most of us want to be team players and do what it takes to excel at our jobs.

By becoming more focused on priorities at work and keeping the Big Picture in mind, you can get more done in less time. Think about how incredibly productive you are the day before you leave on vacation. You whip through your duties with the precision of a heat-seeking missile. Perhaps some of this zeal could carry over to shorter workdays during your regular schedule.

For those who work on a salary, try to set a time you go in to work and a time you leave. Do not leave your departure open-ended, so that a dozen people can stop by your desk to chat or ask a question or tell you the latest office gossip, keeping you at the office while your family is getting ready for bed. While you must be flexible, most of us benefit from a plan for our work schedules.

In tough economic times, businesses run leaner, with fewer folks and tougher standards. Work can swallow up more hours each day. You may need a spouse or buddy to help hold you accountable to more consistent hours. In this day of computers and e-mail and round-the-clock everything, many people have jobs that could take twenty-four hours a day, seven days a week. Set some sort of workable schedule.

One of the most efficient and best managers I ever worked with was the mother of young children. She had to pick them up at the day care center on time each evening or be charged $10 a minute for each minute she was late. She was able to get more done in her workdays than many of the other managers who did similar work.

I have also seen workers who made sure they were in early and left late, came in on weekends, and generally sacrificed much of their outside life for more hours in the office. They were not necessarily the best workers, nor the most creative. They spent so much time in the office that they lost sight of the community, had personal problems that drained them at work, and sometimes took longer to do a task.

As much as possible, honor your time away from work. Many people have jobs that attract attention when you are in the community. A doctor gets a medical question, a pastor runs into a church member who wants some counseling, or a teacher winds up at the café table next to a problem student's parents. In such situations, be polite and friendly. But if the talk strays too far into work, steer that person to your work setting. Give them a card and ask them to give you a call at the office. Or, write their number and promise to follow up the next day. Tell them you look forward to visiting with them at work.

You will have to keep working on these office issues. Unfortunately, just like training the puppy, you cannot do it once and check it off a list. You aren't laying a driveway here that will harden up immediately and be set for years. The world tries hard to shape us in a way that goes against the life we long for. But consider Ephesians 2:10, "For we are God's workmanship, created in Christ Jesus to do good works, which God prepared in advance for us to do." We need to enjoy the days we have been given and live in a way that reflects God's workmanship in us.

Chapter Eight

ENJOY THE JOURNEY

Encouraging Word: *The result of even small efforts can be downright exhilarating.*
Everyday Step: *Do something fun.*

She's got this gift of knowing that life is supposed to be a happy, outrageous business.—Ellen Gilchrist

Afriend of mine was looking through childhood pictures and started crying, not for her lost youthfulness or slim figure but for her huge smile and cocky look. "I have fun times now," she said, "but they seem so disconnected from my real life." For many people, life holds too few fun moments, filled with things that *should* be done rather than things that *could* be done. Some people mistakenly hold having no time for fun as a badge of honor, symbolic of devoted servanthood and maturity. Others, such as my friend, long to go out and play but have lost their way. Embedded in the promise of abundant life is the promise of a life that is enjoyable, not a life of drudgery and doldrums. The Bible is full of reminders that this day is a gift from God and we are to rejoice in it, be glad in it, and to have fun in it. Learning to have fun again is part of learning to hurry less and worry less. Instead of letting more weighty matters shut fun out of your life, shove the hard stuff aside now and then and give in to fun. Sadly, having fun may be as hard as slowing down and not being anxious. You may find yourself wound so tight that relaxation is rough at first, awkward even. Keep at it until you remember how restful it is to have a great time.

The steps to change can begin to free you right away to have more fun. Your *actions,* even at their most feeble, cause hopeful *reactions.* As your steps become more confident and energetic, the results can be downright exhilarating. As I mentioned, one of the unexpected consequences of my journey was my transforming encounter with God and a new realization that I am supposed to enjoy life, not be ground down by the grind. God wants us to choose a calmer, more enjoyable life and will help us achieve it. Joy in daily life is, after all, woven through the promises of God.

Restored and Renewed

In our hurried world, we often forget these reassurances or think we need to be holy or pass some sort of spiritual test for them to work. A reminder: God does wonderful work in the lives of ordinary people, people just like us who are off-track and need a nudge to get redirected. As I tried to hurry and worry less, I came upon Psalm 51:12: "Restore to me the joy of my salvation / and grant me a willing spirit, to sustain me." The verse stung me. I realized that if I was not enjoying every day, I was not feeling the joy of being a child of God. I began to pray that this would be restored to me and that God would grant me the spirit to sustain that. It was helpful to realize that the psalmist realized, those many centuries ago, the need to sustain the effort. Maintaining this attitude of joy is not like putting a quarter in a machine and getting a piece of gum out. It is about day-in-and-day-out focus and commitment to a new way of living. This needed to permeate every part of my life—but darn was that hard! I kept fighting the tendency to do too much.

Call upon encouragers in your life, people who will hold you accountable to this change.

"Simplify, simplify," my husband would say *again* as I tried to fancy up another family supper or add three stops on a two-day trip. My oldest brother told me to say no to every third invitation or commitment. At first I rolled my eyes—no one could really rule things out that arbitrarily—but then I used his rule of three as a reminder that I did not have to say yes to everything. Such efforts to make changes daily became a sort of game. I began to use some of the energy I had spent overdoing on undoing.

Part of this approach provides the energy to tackle important projects and lighthearted activities that have been too long neglected. You might find yourself going to a movie with your husband or wife or planting that herb garden you have wanted to try or walking down the street to have coffee with a friend.

Part of the joy is how we grow. We begin to realize how important those little missing parts of us are, how we can make time to make changes. In life, we seem to be dissatisfied and stressed sometimes because we are trying to have it all. We do not want to give up one thing to grab onto another— we try to hang onto it all. When you begin to be willing to give up something—even if it means a lot to you—for something more meaningful, your life will become more enjoyable.

Weave Exercise into Your Schedule

At first exercising will seem like yet another item on your to-do list, but it can help you have more energy and feel better each day. I have found consistent exercise to be one of the hardest things to do over the years. It is as though my mind is trying to talk me out of it—another of those little voices. But it is one of the best ways I can spend my time. We rob ourselves of a proven stress reliever (and health improver) when we do not get moving. Take up walking—or running—or join a gym or start swimming or ride your bike. Do not start with grand expectations or plans. Do this one step at a time. (And if you have been on the couch for too long, check with your doctor for guidance first.)

I am absolutely the poster child for "if I can do this, anyone can." I decided at age forty that I was unfit and getting too fat. I could not run a mile at the time, but within a year, I had run two marathons. Going out for a slow jog (or what some would consider a brisk walk) works on my stress like spraying cleaner on grease—it cuts right through so much scum inside me, frees me for a better day, and provides some of those found moments for thought and prayer about better ways to live my life.

Allow Yourself Time for R and R—Reflection and Relaxation

You absolutely cannot go full tilt all the time and be content with your life and work. Look at nature. We are made to need sleep and food, and there is a cycle to life.

If the analogy of nature is just a little too serene for you, compare your need for rest and reflection to your computers at work. Perhaps you have gotten one of those cranky e-mails from your systems' guru telling you that you have too many messages and files and folders on your computer and are slowing the system down. You delete a lot of unnecessary stuff and discover that he or she was absolutely right. The machine works better, quicker, and more as it was intended to work. We humans are like that. We need to reboot from time to time. Most people are universally poor at this. We think we are indispensable or worry about what other people will think or always have something we *should* do.

How do you slow down and build in some reflection time? Plan your work so that you have time off. Get out of the habit of working six and seven days a week. Take vacations that clear your mind and schedule. Schedule a morning or evening quiet time—even if it means setting the dreaded alarm clock a few minutes earlier. Have some fun in life, something that gives you energy. Do not feel guilty for it either. Guilt has a way of taking most of the fun out of fun. If you are like me, you have found yourself getting so busy that even the fun things are not fun. Or, the effort to have fun (being out of the office, getting all the chores done) robs you of the fun. As I was writing this chapter, a client told me about her friend who was dreading going on a cruise because she was so busy at home and work. If you find yourself resenting taking a break because it takes time away from those things you *need* to do, change your perspective. See R and R time as a way to make you a more creative and energetic person. Have some times when you let loose. Use these times to be with people you enjoy, times when you do not worry about work or the future of the world.

My husband and I go to the New Orleans Jazz Festival each year with dear friends from Texas. We have done this for a decade now and find it to be one of the most fun, relaxing times we have each year. We roam, eat lots of good food, and hear fantastic musicians who we would never encounter otherwise. We don't think about our responsibilities during this time. We have been known to stand in the rain singing along with James Taylor or under a crowded tent listening to a young gospel choir. Each year something tries to threaten this fun time—work schedules, children's activities, family and church commitments. But because it is fun and rejuvenating, we keep working it out. Find your own JazzFest and enjoy it.

Start by making a list of at least twenty things you would love to do if you had time. Not one or two. Twenty! Next, commit to do two of them in the next two weeks. Not all twenty, just two. Slowly get in the habit of allowing a few minutes here and there for fun—whether it is hitting golf balls at the driving range or reading a good book or going for a walk after supper with your neighbor. Plan something with your family or friends, like a fun activity where you will not be rushed or impatient. As you recall how much fun it is to have fun, you will also begin to remember creative things you used to do—hobbies you had or dreams you wanted to pursue. As you begin to make regular time for leisure activities, you will gradually relearn how to have fun and will begin to relax even when you are not at play. Regrets will begin to retreat, followed by a deep feeling of relief that your life is in order. All because you had a little fun.

When I work with groups on this assignment, a different feeling begins to break out in the room almost immediately—someone remembers how he used to love to go camping but has not made time for that in years or how she wants to make her child a scrapbook for high school graduation. Someone decides to ride his bike again or plan a dream vacation. A couple of weeks after a recent workshop, a young woman was so delighted that she had connected with her father for a fun visit and had been taken dancing by her husband. Both of these events evolved because she had stopped long enough to plan some fun and had begun to act on her plans.

Be Refreshed

Fun things energize us. They refresh us. They help make us more enthusiastic and enjoyable to be around. It takes very little time to start remembering the fun things that we used to do or that we have wanted to do. Some of these are quite small. When I started thinking about fun, I remembered how much I used to love to go to the library. (It was, I am somewhat embarrassed to admit, the first place I drove myself when I got my driver's license.) I committed to carve out some time to visit my library and wander through every aisle, pulling out books for a new look and trying out different magazines. This particular branch had a beautiful view, and I left feeling rested and ready to face new challenges. When I ask people to make such lists, they nearly always have the same response after just a few minutes: "I don't know why I haven't been doing this already."

A good friend loves gardening and for years tried to carve out a little time and space for her hobby. Finally, after much fretting, she asked her boss to allow her to change her schedule one afternoon a week to take a master gardening course. He was happy to oblige, knowing that she was a committed, hard-working leader. The class has opened an entire new world to her, expanding her passion for gardening into a major joy in her life. This very day, as I write, a bright yellow flower sprang forth from the bulbs she planted in our front yard last year for my birthday. Allowing her time and taking a risk to rearrange her work schedule has made her more creative and happier.

Each November, I get together with about eight college girlfriends for what has become known as our annual "Funfest." These women are teachers, nurses, counselors, full-time volunteers, marketers, and they are busy. During this small break, we tell stories. We act silly. We bare our hearts and tell the highs and lows of the year just past. Each year the headline on the weekend is: I love how much we laugh. Each person's family is happy to give us the time to be away because we come back with our batteries recharged. My brother's neighbor has a "guy's crabbing trip" to the Gulf Coast each year. The participants do not shave. They eat lots of good food and laugh a lot and let loose and have a great time.

Perhaps one of the saddest things about hurrying all the time is that somehow we come to believe that fun is wrong. If we are having too much fun, are too relaxed, then we tend to believe that we must be neglecting something important. I could work in my yard, but I need to go to the grocery store. I would like to stop at that flea market to look at antiques, but I need to get home to pay bills and fold clothes. Where in the world did this come from? We were created to enjoy life, to laugh, and to relax. Learning to relax and rest and reflect is not easy. In fact, it may seem like trying to turn an 18-wheeler—those jerky motions that block traffic and require lots of reverse, forward, reverse, forward, new gear, new gear maneuvers. Sometimes the objects in the mirror are closer than they seem, and they will run over you if you do not slow down. Make the turn and laugh while you are doing it.

Chapter Nine

SEEK GOD'S WILL

Encouraging Word: *God has a perfect plan for your life—a plan you will like!*
Everyday Step: *Ask daily about God's path for you.*

God is not after perfecting me to be a specimen in His showroom; He is getting me to the place where He can use me.—Oswald Chambers

When I was a child, I would occasionally pull a jigsaw puzzle off the toy shelf in my closet and impatiently tackle it. I would look at the picture I was trying to create and begin to shuffle pieces, plunging in without a plan and trying to force certain pieces to fit, even though it was obvious they were in the wrong place. As I got a bit older, I learned to start with the edges and work inward, and the final picture emerged more easily. The ultimate aggravation, though, was when I would get to the very end, only to find a piece or two missing. Despite my best efforts, the picture would never be complete, and I felt somehow cheated.

As an adult, that is the way I have sometimes felt about knowing and doing God's will for my life. I have come up with a preconceived picture to be put together, struggled to make an assortment of pieces fit and then thrown up my hands when I discovered that (a) I did not have the pieces I needed; or (b) I knew the pieces were there but I could not, for the life of me, get them to fit. At the best of times, I tried to piece together a border for my life, hoping that the rest of it would fall into place.

Somewhere along my journey to slow down and to quit worrying so much, I realized that even the small steps I was taking in my life were leading me toward a crucial destination—knowing and doing God's will for my life. God certainly did not want me to scurry about like a crazed person, nor want me worrying about what the day would bring. God did want me to enjoy life, to live a full, not frenzied, life. That was clear. What was not as easy to figure out was what I was really supposed to be *doing* with the rest of my life. That led me to lots of soul-searching about God's will, the kind of work I could do, where we could live, *how* I wanted to live, and how I could have a positive impact on the people God placed in my life.

Some people love puzzles, riddles, and mind games. They will tinker with them for hours, trying to figure out what the answer might be, which piece goes where. Others, like me, do not even want to try to figure out how a puzzle works. I will usually walk away from a riddle or puzzle rather than expend any mental energy on something I know will only frustrate me.

These two approaches are how many of us feel about God's will—and along the way, I experienced both of these attitudes. Some of us might stew over God's plan for us for years, figuring if we can just put the right pieces in the right place at the right time, all will be magically revealed. Others dismiss the plan altogether, certain that it is smoke and mirrors, and are unlikely ever truly to know what they are supposed to do and when.

Thankfully, God's will is not a puzzle with missing pieces. Instead, it is a perfect guide for our lives, a plan that not only

allows us to be our best selves but *requires* us to be our best selves. This guide helps life be so much more enjoyable.

It is a step-by-step process, a custom-designed plan created specifically for our individual lives. Exactly suited for us, it is intended to help us live to our fullest and to become what we were created to become—and to enjoy life along the way. This is offered by the grace of God and is personal, between us and God. (Beware the person who tries to tell you what God's will is for *your* life.)

As I was finishing college and trying to figure out what to do with my life, I began to think I had God's will pretty much figured out: I was supposed to love God above all and love others as myself. If I did this, I figured I would be doing God's will, and it would not matter if I were journalist, wife and mom, preacher, or missionary. I still believe this is the core of living as God wants, but I think that plan manifests itself in individual ways for each of us. Perhaps there are certain things we are called to do that no one else can do—a one-on-one relationship with someone who needs love and care, a project that can change our neighborhood, a great idea just waiting for us to act—something that brings our talents together to meet a need. Maybe, just maybe, God wants to use you and needs you to slow down long enough to get directions.

It scares me to think how easy it is to get so busy that we stop trying to do what God wants us to do. As I got busier and busier through the years, I began to veer off course or stopped paying as much attention to loving God and others. I defaulted to the world's way, rushing, fretting, spending too much of my time and energy on too few of the most important things. I was so busy that I was not considering what I was supposed to do with my life. My world was noisy. My body was tired. My mind was full. That did not leave much time or space for seeking God's way.

When I decided to explore a different way of living, one that was less rushed and more enjoyable, little cracks began to open up inside me and certain steps became clearer. Again, this did not start as a spiritual journey; it started because I was worn out. But an amazing thing happened. I began to realize that God makes many steps crystal clear in our lives. While the specific details of what we are to do may sometimes elude us, certain next steps are always clear: Believe in Christ as your Lord and Savior and seek to live as he wants. Love God and love your neighbor. Surrender to God's control—a tough concept that requires special discipline in matters of money, family, work, and so forth. Consider ways to serve the world about you. Be open to spiritual things. Turn to God in every situation, leaning on and growing in God.

Know this: God absolutely does not want us to live in a numb frenzy, hunkered down under our daily circumstances and wondering if we will make it until retirement or until the house is paid off or until the kids are in college or until something.

God wants us to enjoy each day with a thankful and prayerful heart. Pray regularly and specifically about what God wants you to do. Listen to your gut when it suggests that maybe you are headed in the wrong direction.

As we begin examining ways to renew and refresh our lives, God is already gently pushing us toward God's perfect plan for each of us. One of the amazing things about hurrying less and worrying less is that we begin to open ourselves to God's will. Once we *know,* we can begin to *do.* My journey led me through a daily seeking process where I struggled. I have no doubt that I made it more difficult than it needed to be. I am sure I still do. I prayed many times and often felt God leading me in very specific ways. At other times I felt alone and unsure, wondering if there was indeed a "right" answer and wanting to see the future immediately. Mixed in was the fear of making a mistake.

The process reminded me of my less than stellar attempts to snow ski. When I headed downhill, everything in me wanted to lean back, to resist. But to be a great skier, you must relax and lean *into* the downhill ride. At some point as I zoomed through life, I began to know I needed to lean into what God wanted me to do, not trying to force it, not trying to resist it. And if I fell down, I would somehow get back up with God's help.

Renew Your Mind

Recall again the amazing words from Romans 12:2: "Do not conform any longer to the pattern of this world, but be transformed by the renewing of your mind. Then you will be able to test and approve what God's will is—his good, pleasing and perfect will." It is indeed possible to know God's perfect will for you. The good and perfect will that God has for you is custom-made. This divine plan uses the special gifts you were created with to touch the world in a way that only you can. Notice that the Bible tells us that we must renew our *minds* to know this. That means we need to step back and assess, to poke and prod, to read and pray and journal, and to seek advice from people we trust.

The verse above also tells us that we have to test and approve what God's will is for us, somewhat like hiking on a steep path. Our steps may be tentative as we start out, seeking to get our foothold and feel steady. Once we are sure of the path, we walk more confidently, still needing to stop and assess the trail regularly, watching our step, slowing down when needed. Sometimes we may even have to sit down to catch our breath or overcome our fear of a steep drop.

Be Willing to Wait

Knowing God's will seems like a complicated topic, but it is not indecipherable. While we may not have all the answers, each day we have enough information to move forward with confidence and gratitude. In the "instant" age we live in, we want answers now. Instead, God reminds us regularly that we are to wait for God's own timing. We long for clear and sure answers. Those answers come in surprising and subtle ways that we must be alert not to miss. "I waited patiently for the LORD; / he turned to me and heard my cry," Psalm 40:1 says. Often we may take a small step, feeling as though we are barely moving forward. But God will direct us if we listen and do our best to serve God.

This is not something you do once and then never consider again. In my life, sometimes I have felt so certain, sometimes so unsure. At times it has felt as though God was beginning to reveal God's will to me, but then I doubted. I have, at times, been certain I would never be strong enough to do what I was called to do; at other times, I've been afraid that if I surrendered to God's will I would wind up living in a hut in a Third World country. I obviously was still trying to force my own wrongheaded puzzle piece into a God-shaped hole. Somewhere, though, along the way it happens. We realize that God's plan *is* being shown to us; we begin to act on it, tentatively or boldly, and life becomes so much richer.

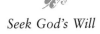

Enjoy a Little Uncertainty

Another step is to realize that a certain amount of uncertainty can indeed be part of what makes life interesting and fulfilling. Whew! This was tough for me to swallow at first, needing and sometimes even demanding quick answers. I was a bit like a child who throws a fit and locks the bedroom door, vowing not to come out until the adults see the error of their ways. As I moved forward, I realized that I would know as I needed to know and that I would have to let that be enough. We seldom get everything laid out for us from start to finish. When my husband and I remodeled an old house, we had a general idea of how we wanted it to look, but things changed along the way. Paint colors looked different on the wall than in the store, the structure of the back wall changed the design and so forth. So it is on my journey.

When I was quite young, someone once told me that life is like a beautiful piece of needlework. When you are living day to day, you see all the threads and knots of the underside and cannot possibly tell how they could create a picture. But when you look back, you see how those very stitches together create a beautiful picture.

CONSIDER THIS: Sometimes things do not go the way we hoped, but instead often turn out much better.

Often we cannot understand why events unfolded as they did. But we pick ourselves up and walk on, overcoming that moment and growing for the moments ahead.

Sometimes We Stumble

Most of us also have stories of times when we thought we were doing God's will—marrying the right person, buying the right home, taking the right job—and it just did not work out. What went wrong? Were we confused about God's will? What about how the Bible tells us that "everything works out for good," or those people who say to everything bad, "It must have been God's will." How do we keep from reducing God's power to a cliché in our lives?

First, "we know that in all things God works for the good *of those who love him, who have been called according to his purpose*" (Romans 8:28, italics added). So, if we are doing God's calling, things will work out for good, some way, somehow, sometimes despite ourselves.

This does not mean that we can avoid bad experiences in life. Instead, it reminds us that God can and does use even painful times and wrong decisions to help us grow. We can continue to mature into the people we were created to be.

Sometimes we will make mistakes, as surely as we take wrong turns on out-of-town trips or stumble in our daily lives. God created us as thinking beings, not puppets. God wants us to be faithful and obedient, but does not make us do anything. That is so liberating—and sometimes so difficult. There have been times when I wished my decisions were made like they are in The Game of Life game, where I spun the little wheel and got instructions on what to do next.

When we make mistakes, we must move on, putting regrets behind us, determined to do better. Philippians 3:13-14 offers a great reminder of this: "Forgetting what is behind and straining toward what is ahead, I press on toward the goal to win the prize for which God has called me heavenward in Christ Jesus."

As you seek God's will in your life, return again and again to the Bible and prayer. God does not play hide-and-seek, hoping we will fail to discover God's presence. Reminders of this abound in God's word, such as Psalm 32:8: "I will instruct you and teach you in the way you should go; / I will counsel you and watch over you." Keep returning to God, no matter how awkward or unsure it feels. If necessary, just sit in a comfortable chair, say, "Here I am, Lord," and wait.

NEXT STEP: Discover your unique gifts.

Perhaps one of the most important steps in knowing God's will is to learn what your special gifts are, the unique ways that God made you, and the ways you might use those gifts. Find a spiritual-gifts course through a local church. Knowing our gifts can help us figure out what God wants us to do. God did not create you this way to try to force you to remake yourself. Some of us are wired to enjoy being with people and to lead and teach. Others prefer quieter days and enjoy building things or praying for others or being there when someone is in need. Study your gifts and use them in a way that helps you shine for God.

TRY THIS: Ask for prayer and feedback from people you trust.

Part of learning God's will is to turn to others for help. If everyone you know thinks that something you are considering is way off base, something may be wrong. Do not gloss over answers that are not what you want to hear. Continue to pray and consider. One of my favorite moments when I was trying to make hard changes in my life came from one of my best friends. "Am I insane?" I asked, fully expecting her to tell me I was the least crazy person she knew. She pondered for a moment. "I don't think so . . ." she replied. Hmm. Maybe I needed to reconsider parts of my plan.

As you try to do God's will, do not neglect those people God has placed in your life. Few of us live in a vacuum. Our decisions affect others and God does not lead us in directions that destroy or harm others. When I was considering quitting my job to start a business, for instance, I had to talk with my husband about it immediately, knowing it would have a huge impact on our daily lives, family finances, and our future. I knew I needed his feedback and his support.

Spending time trying to know God's will and trying to live according to divine guidance can result in a down deep change in the way we approach each day. It can help us greet each day—or at least most days—with anticipation.

This is not a game of chance where the house always wins; instead, God wants us to win. God wants us to enjoy each day, content in our circumstances, living out God's plans. We can know this in a variety of ways, but the best is through repeatedly seeking guidance from the Bible and watching patiently and listening for God's answers to prayer. We can then begin to expect great things and to prepare for them.

TRY THIS: Ask God each day what you are to do—to help you know and do God's will. Ask God to bless your efforts. Thank God for the adventures the day will bring.

We know that Christ came so that we might have life to the fullest. We must also then know that whatever God's plan is for us, God wants us to enjoy life abundantly. If you are not enjoying your daily life, take another look at how you are choosing to live.

Surely God does not want you to be miserable. Consider the wonderful promise in Jeremiah 29:11-13: " 'For I know the plans I have for you,' declares the LORD, 'plans to prosper you and not to harm you, plans to give you hope and a future. Then you will call upon me and come and pray to me, and I will listen to you. You will seek me and find me when you seek me with all your heart.' "

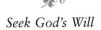

Seek God's Will

God has a plan for us, a plan for a hope and a future. God wants good things to happen to us. God wants us to succeed in a life filled with the right decisions, with plans chosen just for us. But it's perfectly clear that plan does not include hurry and worry.

Chapter Ten

Do Not Give Up

Encouraging Word: *When you start slipping, stop and get back on track.*
Everyday Step: *Pray each day for guidance with your schedule.*

When we die and go to heaven, our Maker is not going to say, why didn't you discover the cure for such and such? The only thing we're going to be asked at that precious moment is why didn't you become you?—Elie Wiesel, paraphrasing Rabbi Zusya

*Y*ou know that living day in and day out with less hurry and less worry requires effort—and on some days seems nearly impossible. As I struggled, I found that I could do it part of the time, then more regularly—but it was tough to be consistent. At certain times, this quest seems like trying to put out a grass fire—just when you have beaten one spot down, another pops up. You can wear yourself out moving from patch to patch.

Over the past few years, I have occasionally felt that my life was once more slipping out of control—usually because I said yes when I should have said no and when I momentarily disregarded how I truly wanted to live. No matter how hard I tried, I could not seem to get my schedule to look the way I wanted it to. I am reminded of a time in my young adult days when I was playing right field in a softball game.

I hurled the ball with all my might, meaning for it to go to home plate. Instead it headed straight to center field. I never was sure how that happened, and sometimes my scheduling feels like that.

Thankfully, I realize that I can get back on track by stopping regularly, assessing what is happening, and focusing on the basics again. After glimpsing how wonderful life can be with less hurry and less worry, I refuse to give up. This does not mean I take a month-long retreat or forsake my job and family. It does mean I carve out a few minutes here and there to figure out what I need to do—and not do.

Know What Causes You to Stumble

As you try to be less tense and tired, it is helpful to notice what is likely to draw you off course and to plan accordingly for that. This will be a bit like knowing that jalapeño peppers always give you heartburn or that new loafers always rub a blister on the top of your foot. You will need to use the strategies you have been building in your everyday life and to recall that you want to enjoy life to the fullest.

As with most important things in life, hurrying less and worrying less requires a commitment to an ongoing way of living. Again, this is not a time-management course or a guide to becoming more efficient. It is about transforming your life, tweaking here and there, taking inventory of the good and bad, and moving ahead. It is not something you do once and check off your to-do list. The path sometimes meanders, sometimes takes a direct route. Continue to focus consistently on your desire to live a more meaningful life, one that is slower, fuller.

When you begin to flounder, stop and *think again* about living differently. Those thoughts will help you *act* differently.

The world may seem to conspire against you and draw you offtrack, making you believe that you cannot possibly live with a renewed and refreshed soul, that you cannot possibly continue to hurry and worry less.

The world is wrong.

God is guiding us on this great adventure with an impeccable sense of direction. Recall the stories of Moses in the Bible, especially how he tried to weasel out of what God wanted him to do, certain that someone (such as his brother) could do it better than he could. As the people wandered in the wilderness, complaining like the worst group of whiners imaginable, God always provided for them, despite their poor attitude and lack of faith. The Creator is your refuge on your journey with promises that will come true.

These efforts do not require you to be perfect. We *are* expected, however, to turn this journey over to God for guidance. This way of living is not impossible. Perhaps you will make your home your sanctuary with a renewed commitment to your family. Perhaps you will set boundaries on your work, certain that just a few more hours in the office are not what you need. Maybe you will find a place to lead as a servant in your church or community, to make the world a better place for those who come behind. We do not have to wait a single moment before starting to improve ourselves and our daily lives.

MORE TIPS TO HELP YOU STAY ON COURSE: Keep the basics of your journey in mind: What do you want your life to look like? Know where you are headed. Get directions for your trip.

Lean on God constantly in prayer. You might start each

day with this prayer from Psalm 5:3: "In the morning, O LORD, you hear my voice; / in the morning I lay my requests before you / and wait in expectation."

Remember, then, to anticipate what the day will bring and to expect God's blessings to be heaped upon you. When you begin to lose your way, recall what you want for your life and that God is in control. Give up worry.

Live gratefully. Be thankful for all the good things that have come your way and all the bad things that did not happen.

Ask others for help. I love the story in 2 Timothy 4 where Paul, one of the great leaders of the Christian faith, is in prison and asks his young friend Timothy for a favor. He wants Timothy to come quickly and to bring Mark and his cloak and his scrolls, very specific and personal requests. We can ask the same of our friends, family, and colleagues. We can ask for guidance and for them to hold us accountable when they notice us beginning to live in a tizzy.

Shortly after I started my business, with this passage in mind, I began to ask people to pray for me. I was excited and anxious about taking such a big step. As the prayers began, I immediately felt God's calming presence. Do not hesitate to ask trusted people to pray for you.

Losing Track of Your Schedule

Each of us is different, but many of us get offtrack with the same sorts of things—particularly piling too many activities onto our calendars, wasting time on activities that do not match our priorities, and obsessing over daily happenings that are simply not that important.

Nearly everyone I know loses control of his or her schedule during the holidays. But something about the season between Thanksgiving and Christmas brings out the worst in most schedules and schedulers. A major dose of hurry and worry often is served up with our fantasies of perfect traditions and juggling home, work, church, and relatives. To enjoy the holidays fully usually requires scheduling conservatively, avoiding the urge to pack each minute of each day full.

During the holidays, the world seems to turn up the volume on its demands—do more, spend more, eat more. Take a few moments before Thanksgiving to write down what you would like your holidays to look like. List a half dozen or so things you want to be sure to do over the holidays—ranging from a Christmas lunch with your best friends to carving out time to take the children to see Christmas lights. Then, list two or three activities that cause you stress that you can toss from your schedule.

Other triggers for some folks include milestones such as graduation, weddings, retirements, and annual events such as back-to-school. Try to plan for these events with a simple timeline. Allow yourself time to prepare; do not wait until the last minute or try to do too much. For special events, focus on the meaning of these occasions and do not fret about all the extras. Know, too, that transitions often bring worries and are Seasons of Time that need special attention.

Enjoy Each Day

Our time is given to us minute by minute. We can no more save it than the Israelites could hoard the manna while wandering in the desert. We instead have to use it fully each day. On the days when you feel like you are spiraling out of control, simply pause. Take a deep breath. Decide to enjoy that one day. Tomorrow will be a new day to consider.

Each of us has a unique journey, full of hope. Carry the words of Ephesians 4:1 in your heart as you strive to hurry less and worry less, remembering to "live a life worthy of the calling you have received." This calling is for a rich and wonderful life—a life faithful to God and dependent on God to help us move forward.

I have become increasingly convinced that we are put on this earth to be totally, wholly us, uniquely created to be used by God somehow to make this world a better place. I do not sense that this means I should run for president or find the cure for cancer. I know in my heart it means living each day fully, not "what if-ing" about what might go wrong, not doing so much each day that I am instead actually doing very little that matters.

A sense of excitement grows within me with the realization that God's plans for us are tremendous. Our Lord will bless us well beyond what we can imagine if we are willing to listen and respond. God wants us to live with a joyful, thankful heart.

Keep at it. The results are definitely worth the effort.

Resources to Help You Along the Way

*A*s you learn to hurry less and worry less, you will need regular inspiration to keep you moving forward. Pick and choose the resources that work for you.

Start a Hurry-Less, Worry-Less Small Group

Invite a few friends to join you on the journey. Almost everyone struggles with too much to do and too little time, so you should have little trouble finding folks who need the class. The challenge will be finding just the right time and format to entice busy people to slow down. Since everyone is busy, keep meetings short, forty-five minutes to an hour. Consider meeting every other week, and limit the total number of weeks the group will meet. (If the group grows close and wants to continue, that is great. But most busy people like to know up front what sort of time commitment is involved.)

Use this book as a study guide. Ask members to read a chapter in advance when possible and jot down thoughts at home. Then, discuss the results. I have found that many people not only want to talk about these issues, they need to talk about them. Inspiration—and determination to live more fully—will come from one another. The group can tackle these issues together and help one another stay on track.

Start the Journey with a Friend

Perhaps you do not want to add another meeting or study group to your schedule. One possibility is to enjoy this process with one of your friends, perhaps someone you have wanted to see more of but could not find time for. Commit together to read the book and do the exercises. Then discuss them casually. Try meeting for lunch, for example, or taking a walk around the block before or after work. (You will not only be moving forward in shaping your life, but also getting in shape!) Or, talk about it over coffee while your children play together or while watching a soccer game or ballet practice or waiting for swim lessons to end.

You might choose to have an e-mail correspondence with an out-of-town friend where you chat briefly about the issues you are each facing and how you are moving forward. Encourage each other!

Study Questions for Groups or Individuals

As you dive into each chapter and begin to think about your individual strategies to live more meaningfully, the following questions may spark thoughts and new ideas. Consider these anew with each chapter, noticing your progress and celebrating it:

1. What did you learn about yourself in this chapter?
2. Were there any surprises?
3. What is working well in your life at this moment? What needs tweaking?
4. What roadblocks are keeping you from hurrying less and worrying less today?

5. What might you do to remove some of these roadblocks?
6. What nagging problems are limiting your control of your schedule?
7. What are some steps to tackle those nagging problems?
8. What two or three small steps could you take to move forward in the next few days?
9. What is one thing you feel really good about in your life right now?
10. What progress have you made on your journey to hurry less and worry less?

Keep a Journal

Whether you choose to move forward alone or with a group, a journal can be a very helpful resource. You do not have to write every day. You are not looking for great literary prose to share with the world. Instead, use your journal to "download your brain," examining what is working in your life and what is not. From this, ideas and solutions unique to your life will pop up. If writing does not come easily to you, consider using your journal for making lists such as these: Why I am hurrying so much this week; ten things I want to do this year; ways I could make my daily work more enjoyable; why I am so tired today, and so forth.

Read, Read, Read

Great ideas will jump out at you from the right book or magazine article at the right time. Plus, reading allows you a few minutes to slow down and can give you energy to get more done later. My life has been immensely enhanced by reading great books.

You will likely come across many books that inspire and teach you, and I would love to hear from you about those. Trying to come up with a short list to help you get started is tough, but here are a few that have been helpful to me:

The Path: Creating Your Mission Statement for Work and for Life
by Laurie Beth Jones (Hyperion, 1996)

The author offers advice on how to define and fulfill a mission. Two of my favorite parts of this book are about a half dozen pages of verbs to help you determine your gifts and an assignment that helps you figure out what most interests you in life. I found that simple exercise to be quite helpful. Jones also offers a variety of case studies (most from the Bible) and questions to consider. An example is: "What would you do if you were ten times bolder? Go out, and do it." This is one of the books that I have given to several friends who are searching for or fine-tuning their mission in life.

Write It Down, Make It Happen: Knowing What You Want—and Getting It!
by Henriette Anne Klauser (Scribner, 2000)

I have kept a diary or journal for thirty-five years or so, so maybe I am prejudiced toward the concept, but this is a good book if you are trying to move forward and make things happen. I have tried this experiment, and it works. I have written it down and it has happened—although I believe prayer needs to be a component of that process. I've told friends about it, and it has worked for them.

This is a book of stories—including stories about people who have written their very specific goals and achieved them. It also opens the door for you to write your own story by coming up with goals and specific things you want to see in your life. Klauser believes that by figuring out what you want and writing it down, you can help miracles occur. I think when we add prayer to this process, miracles do occur! A friend in the newspaper business gave me this book, and I have given away several copies of it. It's a fun, uplifting read with lots of good ideas.

My Utmost for His Highest
by Oswald Chambers (Dodd, Mead & Company, 1935)

I have referred to this devotional classic already and highly recommend it as part of your resource library, ready to be picked up on a day when you feel the urge. This book combines a Scripture verse and short essay for each day of the year and contains much wisdom and thought-provoking sentences. Use this book to build some quiet time into your daily routine. My copy was inscribed by a friend in 1989: "My prayers go with you that the Lord will continue to work in and through you." I offer that blessing to you, too.

Sabbath: Finding Rest, Renewal, and Delight in Our Busy Lives
by Wayne Muller (Bantam Books, 1999)

Muller uses stories and personal experiences to show how to make time to refresh body and mind. This is one of those books you can pick up again and again when you find yourself beginning to be rushed and resentful.

A Place Called Simplicity: The Quiet Beauty of Simple Living
by Claire Cloninger (Harvest House Publishers, 1993)

As I was just beginning to think about a journey to a less hurried way of life, I came across this book about Claire

Cloninger's search for simplicity. Her personal stories and tips were extremely helpful and sparked all sorts of new thoughts for me.

Ordering Your Private World
by Gordon MacDonald (Oliver Nelson, 1985)

This was another book that nearly flew off the shelf and into my mind, and I highly recommend it. It made me realize that many people were struggling with the same sorts of issues I was and that there might indeed be a better way to live.

Gratitude: Affirming the Good Things in Life
by Melody Beattie (MJF Books, 2000)

This is a small book full of large thoughts. Beattie goes well beyond reminding us to give thanks each day for the good things in our lives. She includes a chapter on goal-setting and making each of your challenges into a goal. This is another of those books you will want to leave lying out so you can pick it up for instant inspiration.

The Practice of the Presence of God
by Brother Lawrence (Whitaker House, 1982)

The writings in this little book are about three hundred years old and extremely helpful as you learn to listen to God and develop a deeper awareness of God.

Devotional Classics
edited by Richard J. Foster and James Bryan Smith (HarperSanFrancisco, 1993)

This book is a great spiritual resource as you become more interested in Bible study and quiet time. It contains fifty-two selections by great devotional writers, and reflections and exercises to take you further.

Synchronicity: The Inner Path of Leadership
by Joseph Jaworski (Berrett-Koehler Publishers, 1998)

Among other things, this book can help you think about shaping your future as a leader. It has personal and professional applications.

The Power of Full Engagement: Managing Energy, Not Time, Is the Key to High Performance and Personal Renewal
by Jim Loehr and Tony Schwartz (Free Press, 2003)

This is more of a business book, but it also integrates your personal life. As the title suggests, this book explains that we can't really manage time; we must manage our energy, both on and off the job. A step-by-step program includes an assessment to determine how fully engaged you are. I found it to be an interesting look from a slightly different angle at this business of balancing our lives and having the energy and focus to do what we want and need to do.

Tell Me Your Story

I would love to hear about your journey and ways you have learned to hurry less and worry less, tips for others and ongoing challenges. Please e-mail me at judy@judypchristie.com or write to me at 3218 Line Avenue, Suite 222, Shreveport, LA 71104.